Signs in the Heavens

Unlocking the Secrets of the Zodiac & Heavenly Bodies

By Robert Rite

Table of Contents

Get Complimentary Access to: "Prophecy Alerts"

Dear Reader: Prophecies are being fulfilled so rapidly in these last days that I am offering my readers complimentary access to *"prophecy alerts"* so that you get "*Breaking Prophecy News*" as soon as it breaks...Just follow this link below and sign Up today...
http://robertritebooks.com/prophecy-alerts/

Chapter 1: The Heavens Declare the Glory of God

"The heavens declare the glory of God and the firmament shows His handiwork. Day unto day utters speech and night unto night shows knowledge" (Psalms 19: 1-2)

Since the dawn of this age man has been fascinated by the magnificent beauty of the heavens. It appears that the twelve Zodiac signs have existed from the beginning when God said **"let them be for signs"**. All religions, ancient artifacts, hieroglyphics, and civilizations since before the written word, have the exact same twelve signs, in the exact same order, and with the same image! It's as if they were planted in the heavens with a manual that labeled each one of them for us.

The ancient Arabians and Persians all credit the mapping of the Zodiac to the descendants of Adam; primarily Seth and Enoch. The Zodiac is a ring of twelve star groups called constellations that are organized in such a manner as to form images or pictures. Each one was ascribed a name and was given a divine picture or story behind them. Following are the names of each of these constellations: Virgo, Libra, Scorpio, Sagittarius, Capricorn, Aquarius, Pisces, Aries, Taurus, Gemini, Cancer, Leo.

In this book you will discover how and why the true meaning behind the major constellations (the Zodiac) has been concealed for thousands of years, and how new signs in the sky starting in 2014 may signal turbulent times ahead for mankind.

The zodiac signs (12 constellations) displayed in the heavens from the dawn of creation, reveal many divine secrets. And God also makes mention of some of these signs Himself. Astronomy is the science of studying the movements of the stars and planets and that is acceptable to God. God Himself calls the stars all by name (**Psalm 147:4**), and tells us that heavens were created for the telling of time and seasons, as well as for signs (**Genesis 1:14**).

Astrology is an occult practice deceiving mankind into believing that the zodiac can guide or predict their future. You should not look up to the stars for advice. You should only look to God and the bible for advice.

But these heavenly bodies are not to be worshipped as the astrologers, idol worshippers, and other occult practitioners do. God warned mankind of this very thing in **Deuteronomy 4:19**: *"And take heed, lest you lift your eyes to heaven, and when you see the sun, the moon, and the stars, all the host of heaven, you feel driven to worship them and serve them, which the Lord your God has given to all the peoples under the whole heaven as a heritage."*

Indeed, many foolishly worship the creation instead of the creator! Astrology uses the zodiac in a corrupted form due to Satanic influence to confuse the masses and to hide the truth that God displayed in the heavens for all to see!

Astrology is an occult practice deceiving mankind into believing that the zodiac can guide or predict their future. You should not look up to the stars for advice. You should only look to God and the bible for advice.

The message of the zodiac when distorted by astrology is indeed PAGAN? It is associated with many false gods, and goddesses from Egyptian, Babylonian; Greek and Roman mythology. The signs of the zodiac have been corrupted by heathen astrology but the truth behind the symbols has never changed. The Zodiac indeed BECAME corrupted, just as our sinful nature corrupts just about every truth that the Lord establishes.

The prince of this world (Satan) wants us to think that the Zodiac and the signs in the heavens all originated from Mythology, folklore and the occult. He does not want us to unlock these heavenly truths. What has been masqueraded and perverted by the occult practices such as Astrology, are really hidden signs and messages that almighty God placed in the heavens for His elect throughout this age to discern. We are His elect - when we seek God out and find Him! Satan desperately seeks to conceal the true message contained in the signs of the zodiac - he does NOT want you to discover which side wins!

There are many signs for us to discern in God's great billboard in the sky (the universe). The more we study these signs, the more heavenly secrets are revealed to us. The truth of God was posted in the heavens long before the written word, as a testimony of the sovereignty, omnipotence and the glory of God Almighty. God's bible was written in the night sky long before the dawn of this age!

The Zodiac appears to be the earliest revelation from God to mankind; in hi definition picture form because at that time the word in print did not yet exist! Each of the 12 signs is a picture of future prophetic events that would gradually unfold throughout the age of man. It is a big picture of God's plan and purpose for this age.

There are twelve major zodiac signs (constellations) in the heavens and amazingly these 12 zodiac signs are recognized by every nation and kingdom since the dawn of this age. It is believed by some that these zodiac signs predate any other writings. Even the Persians and Arabians credit the identification of these signs to Adam, Seth and Enoch of the Old Testament! I will show you in this book, how It appears that the 12 signs of the zodiac are from God Himself.

Now before you call me a heretic, I refer to the oldest book of the bible. Long before Abraham or Moses walked the earth, and before Homer wrote his Odyssey and Iliad, we find evidence of the divine significance of the zodiac signs in the oldest book in the bible which is actually the book of Job. After persevering great trials, God intervenes. But first He enlightens Job with many divine truths. In **Job 38:31-33** God declares the following:

"Can you bind the cluster of the Pleiades, or loose the belt of Orion? Can you bring out Mazzaroth in its season? Or can you guide the Great Bear with its cubs? Do you know the ordinances of the heavens? Can you set their dominion over the earth?"

<u>Very Important</u>: In the above passage, God is making reference to "Mazzaroth". Mazzaroth is a Hebrew term for: "the Constellations of the Zodiac"! God here is confirming the antiquity and authenticity of the zodiac as scriptural signs! Mankind influenced by Satan, has distorted the truth behind all of the signs in order to align them with the myths, false gods, goddesses and other idols of the ancient Greeks, Babylonian and other early civilizations.

He also makes reference to the constellations: Orion, Pleiades and Arcturus. In the book of Job we also find references to other constellations including:
- Cetus, the sea monster (referred to as Leviathan)
- Draco, the great dragon

The prophet Amos makes reference to the constellation Orion in the following verse: "Seek Him that makes the seven stars and Orion" (Amos 5: 8).

Indeed, God created the star groups called the Zodiac. The bible refers to these signs in the night sky as the MAZZAROTH. These signs reveal a wonderful picture of creation and redemption. They reflect the ongoing battles between the prince of this world, and the God of heaven - between the serpent and the Lion of the tribe of Judah. The zodiac as well as all prophecy points to Jesus Christ as the King of the Universe! These affirm the revelation of the word contained in the bible. As Revelation declares: "...For the testimony of Jesus is the spirit of prophecy" **Revelation 19:10.**

Other Bible References to the Zodiac/Constellations:

Virgo - Revelation 12:1-2,5
Draco the Dragon - Revelation 12:3
Venus (Isa. 14: 12);
Saturn (Amos 5: 26);
the Pleiades (Job 9: 9; 38: 31; Amos 5: 8);
Orion (Job 38: 31; Amos 5: 8);
Arcturus (Job 9: 9; 38: 32) ;
the twelve signs of the Zodiac (Job 38: 32-33; Isa. 13: 10; Judges 5: 20).
Isaiah 27: 1; Isaiah 13:10; Job 41: 1; Job 26: 13; Ps. 104: 25-26; Psalm 9:1-4; Job 38:31-33

IMPORTANT NOTE: in Job chapters 38 and 39, we are given the twelve Signs of the Zodiac! Battles of heaven -- Job 38: 37; Lions -- Job 38: 39; Ravens -- Job 39: 41; Wild goats -- Job 39: 1; Hinds -- Job 39: 1; Wild ass -- Job 39: 5; Unicorn 39: 9; Peacocks --Job 39.13; Ostrich -- Job 39 :13; Horse -- Job 39 :19; Hawk -- Job 39: 26; Eagle -- Job 39 :27. ***Clearly, the signs of the Zodiac have a divine meaning.***

The constellations (zodiac) display the history of mankind and the ongoing cosmic battle between good and evil. The bible teaches that God Himself has named all the stars: **Psalm 147:4** "He determines **the** number of **the stars** and calls **them** each by name." As you will see this is more proof that the signs of the heavens are signs from God. God reveals this in **Genesis 1:14**: ***"And God said, "Let there be*** *lights in the firmament of the heavens to divide the day from the night, and let them be for signs and seasons, and for days and years."*

The word *"Signs"* here most definitely implies that the heavens may have foretold before the dawn of this age the outcome of that galactic battle between good and evil. The prophecies have been unveiled for us from the beginning of time.

In this book you will understand how each of the twelve of the zodiac signs is a picture of God and prophetic word. Unlike what the astrologers want you to think, your destiny has nothing to do with the month you were born, but rather everything to do with whom you choose to place your trust and faith upon. **Your month of birth is insignificant since, as you shall see, every single zodiac sign reveals a divine truth**.

Pride is one of the deadliest of sins because that is a character trait of Satan who is so full of pride that he refuses to acknowledge that God Almighty rules the universe and that Satan will never win the battle between good and evil. As you will see, four of the zodiac signs clearly reveal the fate of the serpent (Satan).

Sadly, because of our sinful nature many are so full of Satan's pride, as to think that they are gods within themselves and that they do not need to keep God's commandments nor worship the God who grants them the choice to choose, and the breath of life! They presume that since God does not strike them dead because of their rebellious heart, that God is weak, or that He does not exist, or that He is powerless over their lives. They do not understand that Love (God) is very patient!

The heavens declare that the spirit in us and our being as the body of Christ can manifest on earth what is in heaven! We are the embodiment of all the goodness that awaits us when we reunite as a spirit body with our creator. We through the power of the Holy Spirit can manifest what is in the supernatural realm of heaven in the natural world, in the here and now!

The kingdom of heaven should not be this far out of sight place unattainable to mortal man. It indeed dwells inside of us when we are enabled by the power of the Holy Spirit. It is this spirit that allows us to literally experience heaven on earth.

New agers and false prophets are living a deluded half truth when they claim they are gods when in fact the god that they believe in and worship is the god of this world and not the God of heaven. Adam and Even fell for this same deception when they believed the serpent's lie that they would be like God despite disobedience and sin: **Genesis 3:5:** *"For God knows that when you eat from it your eyes will be opened, and you will be like God, knowing good and evil."* Here he seduces them by offering them divine powers in return for their soul. Satan is a master at subtle lies and half truths. In the Garden he tricked Adam out of his inheritance by twisting the truth.

The god that new agers think they are is that god that Satan wants us to worship him. They fail to recognize that there is a big difference between being god and having GOD dwell and empower us through His holy spirit. The former is blasphemy against the Holy Spirit while the later is submission to the authority of God, which leads to eternal life and a host of other blessings and promises.

During Jesus 3 1/2 year ministry he was the suffering Messiah. In the first half of the tribulation period (3 1/2 years) just before His return, we witness in heaven that Jesus is bestowed the crown and title of the *"Lion of the Tribe of Judah"* **Revelation 5:5.**

As you will see, the zodiac signs reveal much. The constellations (zodiac) are indeed God's word displayed in the heavens - these are the signs for this age.
Indeed, all of us have at one time or another pondered the awesome beauty of the heavens with the myriad countless stars and galaxies. It is a testament of the awesome greatness of our God. Many of us have wondered why God would care about our planet which is such a tiny insignificant speck in comparison to the smallest of stars in the Universe. Even more - so why would God care about us who are but a speck of sand in comparison to the size of this earth - let alone the universe. It seems that God shows us how he can do so much with so little - a testament to His glory. The tiny nation of Israel (God's Land) and tiny planet earth (in comparison to the Universe) are clear examples of this. Yet I believe that tiny Israel and tiny earth are the beginnings of God's grand plan for the universe through eternity. Both God's word and the heavenly signs clearly point to this!

The bible declares in **Jeremiah 33:22** that the host (stars) of heaven cannot be numbered. Only in the last 100 years have astronomers confirmed what the bible revealed thousands of years ago, that the number of stars in the universe cannot be counted by man; some estimate however that perhaps one sextillion (that is a 1 followed by 21 zeros) stars exist in the universe - an uncountable number indeed! Yet our awesome creator has named every single star!

Psalm 147:4 *"He counts the number of the stars; He calls them all by name."*
Jeremiah 33:22 *"As the host of heaven cannot be numbered, nor the sand of the sea measured, so will I multiply the descendants of David My servant and the Levites who minister to Me."*

Each Zodiac sign is a picture of one of the following:

1) the Messiah
2) the trials of each believer
3) the schemes of the serpent - Satan
4) the progressive battle between good and evil
5) the church - the body of Christ

In this book, I will unlock many great mysteries for you, including the significance of the **coming blood moons and solar eclipse**. Join me as we span the universe and unlock the many mysteries in the heavens. This is just the beginning!

Even SCIENCE Declares the Glory of God!

In my quest to understand truth the Lord has blessed me with some words of knowledge that I want to share with you. Despite their quest to discredit God as the Creator, even modern science is now making discoveries that actually confirm that the secrets of the universe were declared by God Almighty before He created science, physics and scientists!

Scientists claim that we are made from the stars and that without supernova there is no life - that our material all originated from star dust. If that is the case then perhaps that is why Jesus declared that he is the **bright morning star!** Indeed, Christ is the star that formed every atom in our body - making us a star child - a child of God!

   "Then He brought him outside and said, "Look now toward heaven, and count the stars if you are able to number them." And He said to him, "So shall your descendants be." Genesis 15:5

"When the morning stars sang together, And all the sons of God shouted for joy?" Job 3:9

"I, Jesus, have sent My angel to testify to you these things in the churches. I am the Root and the Offspring of David, the Bright and Morning Star." **Revelation 22:16**

Scientist's claim that as hydrogen dissipates from the universe eventually all stars will disappear - could that be confirming what God declared thousands of years ago?

*"Now I saw a new heaven and **a new earth, for the first heaven and the first earth had passed away**. Also there was no more sea."* **Revelation 21:1**

Scientists claim that sometime in the future the Universe will become totally dark. Could they unknowingly be confirming what the bible declared thousands of years ago:

*"The city had **no need of the sun** or of the moon to shine in it, for the glory of God illuminated it. The Lamb is its light."* **Revelation 21:23**

Scientists believe that the future of the universe looks grim per their aforementioned discoveries. There will be no need for astronomy in the new age of God either! We are the stars of the new heavens:

***"Those who are wise shall shine Like the brightness of the firmament, And those who turn many to righteousness Like the stars forever and ever."* Daniel 12:3**

If there was a big bang then it must have been God himself who orchestrated it when he said, **let there be light**! A big bang produces light! The universe was once an atom and now it just keeps expanding, just as the body of Christ keeps growing until the full number is reached!

*"I, Jesus, have sent My angel to testify to you these things in the churches. I am the Root and the Offspring of David, the Bright and **Morning Star**."* **Revelation 22:16**

Modern Scientists confirm that man is made of dust, just like
the stars. How marvelous that not only is man made from
dust, but so are the stars, planets and galaxies created from
dust. Apparently all matter emanates from dust. This is an
astronomical fact - not theory. Fallen man has turned
everything to dust, but only God can take dust and create light
and life out of it. **In the beginning God created light; Jesus
is that light - the light and the life of the world:**

*"In the beginning God created the heavens and the
earth. The earth was without form, and void; and
darkness was on the face of the deep. And the Spirit of
God was hovering over the face of the waters. Then God
said, "Let there be light and there was light. and God saw
the light, that it was good;" Genesis 1:1-3*

*"Then Jesus spoke to them again, saying, "I
am the light of the world. He who follows Me shall not
walk in darkness, but have the light of life." John 8:12
"Jesus said to her, "I am the resurrection and the life. He
who believes in Me, though he may die, he shall live."
John 11:25*

*"Before the mountains were brought forth, or ever You
had formed the earth and the world, even from everlasting
to everlasting, Thou art God. Psalm 90:2*
**The Divine Correlation between the 12 tribes of Israel and
the Zodiac signs:**

In the Jewish temple service the following occurs. Around the
tabernacle were twelve tribes, each bearing a unique standard
or ensign. If you walked around the tabernacle, passing
through each of the twelve tribes, **you would pass through
twelve standards or ensigns**. This matches the twelve signs
of the Zodiac! The twelve ensigns of the twelve tribes of Israel

actually correspond to the configurations of the twelve signs of the Zodiac in the heavens!

The signs of the Zodiac are the route that the sun takes (passes through) as it travels through the heavens. "Tabernacle" means "house". The signs of the Zodiac are called the *"houses"* of the sun, because the sun passes through each one for one month every year.

As we have discussed the sun, moon and stars are for signs. *Jesus is a symbol of the Sun, since He is the son of righteousness who brings light and life to the world!*

The church (the body of Christ) can be equated to the stars in the heavens, since we are the house that the Son of God passes through. God likened the seed of Abraham like the stars of heaven, and there are many other references that I have made throughout this book regarding that relationship.

The Zodiac, Idol Worship and the Occult

The first chapter of Genesis is all about God, and he is mentioned thirty-two times in just this chapter. The bible starts out with these specific words: **"In the beginning, God created the heavens and the earth"** Genesis 1:1. From the very beginning, God wants there to be no confusion about His deity. The God of Abraham, Isaac, and Jacob makes this clear throughout the bible including in **Isaiah 45:6** - *"That they may know from the rising of the sun to its setting That there is none besides Me. I am the Lord, and there is no other;"* God brings this message home several times including: Deuteronomy 4:35; Isaiah 45:21; Isaiah 46:9; Isaiah 44:6; Isaiah 44:24.

So there is ONLY one God, but one of the first things Satan did was to corrupt the meaning of the Zodiac signs to create several mythical gods, idols, and heroes to confuse mankind that there are many gods.

The Zodiac pre-dates Egypt, Babylon, Greece, Rome and all the gods and mythologies of the pagan nations. After the original meanings of the heavenly signs relayed to Adam and his descendants faded from mankind's memory, the carnal mind replaced the truth with fantasy stories based on superstitions and whatever imaginations they held in those days. Many already worshipped the Sun and the Moon and made Gods out of them and out of the stars (much to the devil's delight). Lacking any benefit from the written word, their creative minds were easy prey to Satan's influence.

Satan perverted the practice of observing the universe for the telling of times and signs, into fortune telling and other occult practices designed to get people to seek guidance and make decisions based on channels controlled by Satan, over the word in the bible and God.
As already mentioned, astrology is an occult practice deceiving mankind into believing that the zodiac can predict their future and destiny. You should not look up to the stars for advice. You should only look upon God and the word for advice.

Astrology has no answers it is all based on mythology, folklore, and idolatry. It points to problems and circumstance but offers no conclusions or solutions. It is a science based on delusion and falsehood. God warns about this in **Jeremiah 10:2 - "Do not learn the way of the Gentiles; do not be dismayed at the signs of heaven, for the Gentiles are dismayed at them."**

God makes it very clear how foolish it is to embrace such folly in **Isaiah 47:13 - "You are wearied in the multitude of your counsels; let now the astrologers, the stargazers, and the** *monthly prognosticators stand up and save you from what shall come upon you."*

Now that we have the benefit of divine truth from the old and new testament scriptures, one would think that we would acknowledge the true meaning behind the signs. Yet incredibly, most folks still ignorantly believe in astrology, and all of the mythology associated with the zodiac. Many remain "intrigued" and continue to embrace the mythological version of the meaning behind each zodiac sign.

Chapter 2 - The Universe inside each of us

In the prior chapter I indicated how the body of Christ (the elect) can be likened to the stars in the heavens. In this chapter I just want to share how our bodies are just a, perhaps even more complex, than even more significant to God than the entire cosmos.

God created man, science, physics including the many atheists and nonbelievers who reject God's omnipotence and sovereignty by questioning His capabilities and authority. They thus relegate the marvels of God's creation to some man-made theories such as 'big bang" and "evolution". They wonder why would the God of the universe care so much about tiny Israel or this tiny planet earth.

Instead of glorifying omnipotent God for the creation of this mind boggling expanse called the universe, many have been misled into believing that one God could not have created so much. They in essence prefer to embrace false doctrines that claim that there are many gods, and many ways to God. **Again this is contrary to what God declares. There is only one God**; only **ONE** creator of the universe:

- **Isaiah 44:6** *"Thus says the Lord, the King of Israel, And his Redeemer, the Lord of hosts: 'I am the First and I am the Last; **Besides Me there is no God**."*
- **Isaiah 44:24:** *"Thus says the Lord, you're Redeemer, and He who formed you from the womb: "I am the Lord, who makes all things, who **stretches out the heavens all alone**, Who spreads abroad the earth **by Myself**;"*

How unfortunate that mankind, including the highly educated, place so much value and trust on carnal knowledge and are thus blinded to the truth as revealed by the word of God. They substitute carnal knowledge for heavenly knowledge (wisdom) which God bestows upon those that place their trust on Him. Remember that every theory formed by the carnal mind (that is not scriptural) is under the influence of the god of this world - and therefore will most likely contradict or distort the word of God.

Now that we got that out of the way, here is some food for thought. When you contemplate the miracle of the human body which contains an innumerable number of cells and billions of moving parts and organisms within, it is not just a marvel, but it is as if the sovereign God of the universe created a mini-universe inside all of us. A microcosm (little world) that is so elaborate, that science will never fully master it - and **MOST DEFINITELY** will _**NEVER**_ be able to replicate it. Indeed, there is a whole universe inside of us. And like the universe, it is all from God and as a result it all belongs to God. The word microcosm here implies that man is a condensed version of the whole universe!

The point I want to make here is that when you behold the miracle of our body, you behold the awesome glory of our creator. The glory of God is not only displayed in the universe and on earth, but inside each of us. God has put his spirit inside each of us. It is that spirit that lets us breathe and think, live and blink. Without God we are nothing but the dust that we came from.

We are composed of a mortal body and an eternal soul. Your choices while in this temporary mortal body will determine where your soul will reside in perpetuity". We may indeed be the hieroglyphic of the universe - and since we are created in His image, God's DNA resides in all of us - either in a pure form or in a corrupted form! Our bodies were originally created with the perfect DNA of God, until original sin allowed Satan to corrupt our DNA and thus bring forth all kinds of sickness and suffering.

So because of this corrupted DNA many allow Satan to plant evil thoughts in their mind, such as that we can be like god even while practicing sin and disobedience to the word. We are not gods, as that is exactly what the serpent wants us to think, so that we persist living in sin thinking that there will never be a day of reckoning. The clay (dust) that we are can never be greater than the creator. It is for our sinful nature that we all must return to the ground.

Genesis 3:19 - "*In the sweat of your face you shall eat bread till you return to the ground, For out of it you were taken; **For dust you are, and to dust you shall return.**"*

God created man twice. What I mean here is that God clearly separated the physical man in us and the spiritual man in us. The spiritual man was created first, and then the physical man was created from the dust of the ground. The spiritual is eternal (representative of heaven) and the physical is mortal (representative of earth). The spiritual man is Holy while the physical man is representative of our sinful nature.

God also gave us two minds:
1) The spiritual, sanctified, redeemed holy Spirit filled mind
2) The physical, carnal, sinful, and corrupted mind

So God created the spiritual man on day six in His very own image: **Genesis 1:26** Then God said, "Let Us make man in Our image, according to Our likeness;...". So our spirit existed before our physical body!

In **Genesis 2:7** we then see that God created physical man. He formed man from the dust of the ground and then he breathed into his nostrils the breath of life (God's spirit in us). Out of the dust of the ground man became a living soul. So in us are a physical body and a spiritual eternal soul. So a portion of God's DNA is in all of us - as we are all destined to become children of God, ***if we so choose***. Can you see how we are such a privileged and unique creation in the universe!

From the above remember the following: Since God created man on the sixth day - the number six is the number of man. God rested on the seventh day - and made it ***Holy***, therefore the number seven is the number of God. It will come in handy later!

Many have been sold into believing another one of Satan's half truths which is the myth of **reincarnation.** This is a demonic distortion of the strong possibility that our spirit man may have existed in heaven before we were placed on earth! **Ephesians 1:4-5 "** *just as He chose us in Him **before the foundation of the world**, that we should be holy and without blame before Him in love, having predestined us to adoption as sons by Jesus Christ to Himself, according to the good pleasure of His will,"*.

Read also Romans 8:2; Ephesians 2:4-10. Strike three for those who think abortion is okay.

The heavens declare the glory of God **Psalm 19:1-4**!

Chapter 3 - Virgo the Virgin

Before we begin covering the signs, I want to cover some points that will help understand the following twelve chapters which address one constellation per chapter. please note that every sign (house) of the zodiac includes a major star group (constellation) and three smaller or minor star groups (also constellations) referred to as "Decans". I will cover most if not all of these Decans as well as the zodiac since they work together as a group to tell a story; to form a complete message.

I want to also clarify something **very important**. The seasons relative to the word of God are based on the Hebrew (Jewish) Calendar. Although Nissan is the first month on the Jewish calendar (March-April), it is a somewhat "complex" calendar in that **the Jewish year actually begins and is celebrated on Rosh Hashanah, the first day of the month of Tishrei** (the anniversary of the creation of Adam and Eve according to Hebrew scholars). This month happens to span **September-October**. So the divine interpretation of the zodiac signs relative to bible prophecy, clearly unlock the mysteries of the zodiac when we realize that the sun begins its cycle every year with the sign of Virgo. **VIRGO begins in August 23 - September 22. The Jewish New Year begins in September!**

As we already discussed, the signs of the zodiac are divided into twelve segments (groups of stars) that are divinely connected to the months as the sun travels the path of the zodiac and returns to the same position every 12 months! It ceremonially begins each year with the sign of Virgo the Virgin and ends with Leo (The Lion of the Tribe of Judah).

All of the signs of the zodiac (referred to as houses) are positioned as a massive circle in our galaxy. The sun passes through one of these signs each and every month. Clearly the sun is representative of the **son of God** who is referred to as the **light of the world**!

Every year the Sun starts its journey through the zodiac beginning with Virgo and ending with LEO, the sequence mimics the bible. The first prophecy of promise concerning the seed of the woman (Virgo) is found in **Genesis 3:15** - the first book of the bible. The Sun ends its journey 12 months later passing through Leo (Jesus). The last book of the bible is Revelation. In **Revelation 5:5** Jesus is crowned as the Lion of the Tribe of Judah - just before the end of this age when he will **CRUSH** the head of the serpent - Satan.

This event takes place in **Revelation 19:11-17** which reveals Jesus triumphant return which quickly defeats Satan and all of the lost souls which chose his mark - which is the mark that rejects God and chooses Satan as their god for this age.

Remember that God said that the signs and the heavenly bodies would be not just for signs but also for the telling of seasons, days, and years. Man's yearly calendar is also broken into 12 months in accordance with the movement of the sun through the zodiac.

So we begin our journey with the first sign - Virgo.

As the sun begins its journey anew every 12 months it first passes through Virgo. The true symbol here is that of a virgin.

The first sign of the zodiac lines up perfectly with **the first "GREAT" prophecy** in the bible and that prophecy was **made by the "GREAT" GOD almighty Himself**!
Genesis 3:15 - "And I will put enmity between you and the

woman, And between your seed and her Seed; He shall bruise your head, And you shall bruise His heel."
The above passage from the creator of the universe is probably the most significant prophecy in the bible. In this prophecy **God promised Satan that although he would inflict great pain and suffering upon the Messiah and his offspring throughout the age, the Messiah would crush Satan's head (his kingdom) at the end of this age! Can I hear a Halleluiah!**

This group of stars is associated with the picture of a young woman with an ear of wheat in one hand and a branch in the other hand. In Hebrew she is called BETHULAH, which means a "virgin," In Latin VIRGO means "the virgin." So clearly Virgo is symbolic with a virgin, and the divine symbol of this sign is the Virgin Mary who bore a son, Messiah Jesus Christ, who is called **"the branch"**! As a confirmation of its meaning, the brightest star in Virgo is called Al Zimach in Arabic, and this means: **"the branch"**. Both the wheat and the branch denote fruitfulness - as in offspring/bearing children.

In one of her hands she is holding a branch. As I already indicated, Jesus is **the branch** and he explained this in the following parable: *"I am the vine, you are the branches: He that abides in me and I in him, the same brings forth much fruit* **(John 15: 5; Zech. 6:12).**

As mentioned this sign is as biblical as a sign can be: it is a picture of a virgin which brings forth a seed. In Genesis 3:15 God's great prophecy uses the word seed: *"And I will put enmity between thee (the serpent) and the woman, and between thy seed and her seed.........***Gen. 3:15.** The seed referred to here is the child Messiah to come out of a virgin, and also the church/body of Christ composed of many seeds. The use of the word seed instead of child is very significant because seed reproduces itself - so that out of one will come many. So the seed here is not just referring to the coming Messiah, but to the church of Christ that springs forth from His seed.

Jesus explained this also in the following parable: *Verily, verily, I say unto you, Except a corn (grain) of wheat fall into the ground and die, it abides alone: but if it dies, it brings forth much fruit" (Jn. 12: 23-24).* Jesus likens himself to a seed that was killed, that by his death many would live. His one seed would bring forth a countless harvest of future sons of God.

To be a virgin means to be pure, undefiled and fully committed to the Messiah. It means to resist the desires of the flesh and the pleasures of this world that the carnal mind lusts after. The Holy Spirit can enable us to be pure and undefiled before god's eyes so that we can become kings and priests before God almighty; **Revelation 5:***10 "And You have made us kings and priests to our God; And we shall reign on the earth."*

This sign is also a calling for God's elect to choose a life of purity like a virgin, so that we can partake in the coming marriage supper of the Lamb of God **II Corinthians 11:2** - *"For I am jealous for you with godly jealousy. For I have betrothed you to one husband that I may present you as a chaste virgin to Christ."*

In Prophecy we also read of the sign of Virgo also in Revelation 12:1-2,5; Psalm 9:1-4; Job 38:31-33; Coma

The first Decan in the sign of Virgo is Coma. The word Coma means *"the desired" or "the Longed For"*. The ancient Egyptians referred to this constellation as **Shes-Nu**, which means "**the desired Son**".

So Coma is the picture of a woman admiring a baby in her arms. It is also the woman in Revelation chapter 12. The divine interpretation here is that the child that the virgin is embracing is Messiah Jesus. Jesus is referred to as "*the desire*" in Hag. 2:7. It is also a dual representation of the seed of Jesus, the manifest sons of God; the elect - the church and body of Christ.

Centaurus

We now move on to the second Decan of Virgo - **Centaurus**. This is the picture of a creature having the head and torso of a man, but the legs are of a horse. The ancients believed that Centaurs were begotten from heaven, but they were hated by men and their mythical gods. The ancient's that practiced mythology believed that the **Centaur** was to be exterminated!

The Centaur here is pictured going forth like a hunter. He kills a beast called Victim with his spear. This conflict occurs in the background of the Southern Cross. The name of this constellation in Arabic, Chaldaic and Hebrew was **BEZEH**, which means **"the despised one"**. Wow - this is the exact opposite of Coma, which means "**the desired one**." Yet they are one and the same!

This title **BEZEH** (the despised one) is found several times in the Old Testament. In **Isaiah 53:3** we read:

He is despised and rejected by men, a Man of sorrows and acquainted with grief. and we hid, as it were, our faces from Him; He was despised, and we did not esteem Him.

So this sign is confirming the age old fact that mankind and most of the nations on earth (NOT just Israel) have rejected and despised Messiah Jesus Christ. Even many who claim they are "**Christians**" will never openly admit that they are, choosing instead to conveniently hide under the Satanic inspired umbrella that distorts "justice" with unrighteous laws, such as the separation of church (God) and state (Babylon and its Antichrist world system).

These man-made statutes are the root of all evil laws such as abortion, same sex marriage and many other acts that God ordained as abominations and perversions - yet mankind protects them under the **"law of the land"**. It is this "law of the land" that brings forth the coming apocalypse that will be discussed later on in this book. ***This is because the "law of the land" is what compels fallen man to worship their leaders and their government over God, de facto rejecting and despising the Messiah!***

My brothers and Sisters I share a bittersweet truth - **the freedom that so many peoples, nations, and tongues worship today - may indeed be the freedom from being accountable to sin and God**!

The message behind the Centaur is clear. We must subdue that "Victim" which is representative of the bondage of sin inside us all, and that the world lusts for, by instead desiring and choosing the Messiah - the despised one that most in this fallen world have rejected!

Let's move on now to the Constellation - Libra.

Chapter 4 - Libra the Scales

Our journey through the cosmos now takes us to the star group Libra.

In Latin Libra means "**the scales**". In Hebrew Libra is MOZANAIM, which translates to "**the scales weighing**." Libra is a symbol of antique scales - the kind that work like a seesaw. These types of scales were first used by the Egyptians to weigh items. On one scale the item would be placed and on the other stones that would determine the weight of the item once the scales are balanced. Egyptian, Greek and Indian mythology all also considers Libra to represent scales, but all have different meanings. Scales today are a symbol of justice.

One of the scales is lifted higher. This scale represents **Jesus Christ** because the **star connected** to this scale is called *"the price which covers"*. The blood of Jesus at the cross is: "the **price** which **covers**" our sins! Isn't this so amazing!

This sign is symbolic of the importance of balance in all of God's creation; not just in the Cosmos, but inside each of us. Balance is essential to sustain life. For example, our sun is perfectly positioned (balanced) to sustain life on earth.

Spiritually, a lack of balance leads to sin - so we must keep our carnal mind and sinful nature in check. Self control is one of the fruits of the Holy Spirit read II Peter 1:4-8. Jesus is the perfect example of perfect balance. As we mature as Christians our life can also become perfectly balanced.

God is one - he is not divisible! He is perfect balance. He is love. There is ONLY one God! If there was more than one God (like Satan attempted to establish) then the Universe could not be in perfect balance!

So balance is a universal law created by the creator of all things:

- There must be darkness in order for there to be light
- There must exist sin is there is to be redemption
- There must be death if there is to be eternal life
- There must exist evil and hatred if there is to exist good and love
- There must exist judgment and punishment if there is to be cleansing and rebalancing

The Southern Cross:

The first of Libra's **Decans** (minor constellations) is called **The Southern Cross**. Located beneath the feet of a Centaur. This minor constellation is very beautiful; Consisting of 4 bright stars in the form of a cross. At the time of the *Messiah Christ's birth this star group was actually position in the same latitude as Bethlehem*! Could this be the star that led the Magi to the manger?

In Hebrew The Southern Cross is referred to as **Adom**, which means **"the cutting off"**. Although they do not know this "yet", the Messiah Jesus would be "cut off" rejected and killed by his own people. This was prophesied to happen in **Daniel 9:26**: "And after the sixty-two weeks Messiah shall be cut off, but not for Himself....".

Jesus death at Calvary (the cross) has made it possible for all mankind to balance their own scales and earn passage to paradise through the blood of the Lamb of God that washes away the sins of the world.

Upon Jesus sacrifice at the cross, something as horrific and cruel as a crucifixion was converted into a Holy symbol of perfect love and sacrifice. It became an instrument of redemption, salvation and the gateway to eternal life! **This picture of the redemptive sacrifice at the cross was placed in the cosmos by our creator many eons before that infamous event in Jerusalem!**

From that cross flows enormous glory and power for eternity. This is clearly expressed in **Revelation 5:12**: "*saying with a loud voice: "Worthy is the Lamb who was slain to receive power and riches and wisdom, and strength and honor and glory and blessing!"* Because of Jesus death at the cross, these same seven blessings are passed on to His elect, the future children of God! These are those who accept Jesus as their Lord and savior and through repentance, they enable the power of the Holy Spirit in their life.

Indeed, Jesus was predestined to be slain at the time God created the heavens and the signs thereof - hence "**The Southern Cross**! He was the firstborn. The proverbs clearly establish that **Jesus was the first creation and existed from the very beginning**.

Proverbs 8:23-31: "*I have been established from everlasting, from the beginning, before there was ever an earth. when there were no depths I was brought forth, when there were no fountains abounding with water. Before the mountains were settled, before the hills, I was brought forth; While as yet He had not made the earth or the fields, or the primal dust of the world. When He prepared the heavens, I was there, When He drew a circle on the face of the deep, when He established the clouds above, when He strengthened the fountains of the deep, when He assigned to the sea its limit, so that the waters would not transgress His command, when He marked out the foundations of the earth, Then I was beside Him as a master craftsman; and I was*

daily His delight,
rejoicing always before Him, rejoicing in His inhabited world,
and my delight was with the sons of men."

Jesus is the light of the world from the beginning, this is why in the beginning God said "Let there be light, and there was light" **Genesis 1:3**! Light is life - that is why we have no need for the signs in the heavens during the daylight for the **son** of God is the light that covers the signs when the light shines upon the world!

Jesus is the word and the word was from the beginning. The signs in the heavens confirm this. The gospel of John clearly explains that the Messiah is the word.

John 1:1-14:
"In the beginning was the Word, and the Word was with God, and the Word was God.
He was in the beginning with God. All things were made through Him, and without Him nothing was made that were made.
In Him was life, and the life was the light of men.
And the light shines in the darkness, and the darkness did not comprehend it. There was a man sent from God, whose name was John.
This man came for a witness, to bear witness of the Light that all through him might believe.
He was not that Light, but was sent to bear witness of that Light.
That was the true Light which gives light to every man coming into the world.
He was in the world, and the world was made through Him, and the world did not know Him. He came to His own, and His own did not receive Him.

But as many as received Him, to them He gave the right to become children of God, to those who believe in His name: who were born, not of blood, nor of the will of the flesh, nor of the will of man, but of God.
And the Word became flesh and dwelt among us, and we beheld His glory, the glory as of the only begotten of the Father, full of grace and truth."

The Northern Crown - the Crown

Another of the Decans of Libra is called **Corona Borealis** which means **"The Northern Crown"**, or **"The Crown"**. In Hebrew it is referred to as **Atarah** which means **"Royal Crown"**. In the Arabic it means **"Jewel"**. We read of this crown in **Isaiah 28:5 - *"In that day the Lord of hosts will be for a crown of glory and a diadem of beauty to the remnant of His people"***

This crown represents the crown of victory worn by the firstborn of the church of God - Jesus Christ. The crown not only belongs to Jesus but to His elect - His seed - the body of Christ (the Church).

We too can become heirs of this crown of victory.
Life is a race against time, and he who wins the race is he who masters the truth and the wisdom of God! Thus it is infinitely better to win the "heavenly" crown of victory which is an everlasting crown, than any earthly crown of success or accomplishment - which is a temporary crown. All who persevere are given a crown of victory from God!
This is an incorruptible crown (which lasts forever), unlike the awards and fame on earth.

We are to be His priests not just in the hereafter, but in the now. So why not start wearing that crown by your good works on earth.

There are different crowns such as the crowns of: Life, Righteousness, Mercy; Glory; and Compassion. God judges and awards fairly. All the good deeds that we do on earth are remembered in heaven.

Indeed Jesus is the key to receiving the **Crown of Victory** that grants us entrance into paradise. Here just a few references to that point:

John 3:16; Revelation 3:11; Rev. 2:7; Rev. 2:10; Luke 9:23; Galatians 5:24; II Corinthians 9:24-25; James 1:12; I Corinthians 15:53-54; John 5:25; Romans 6:23; Phil. 3:7-12; II Timothy 4:7-8; Rev. 20:6; 1 Peter 5:4; Psalm 104:4

Chapter 5 - SCORPIO the Scorpion

This third sign in the Zodiac is the most brilliant of the twelve Zodiac constellations. A picture of a giant scorpion with its tail lifted - signifying that it is angry and ready to attack. Scorpion is a very dangerous and aggressive insect with a very powerful sting that can inflict great pain and suffering - in some cases death. It is attempting to sting a man in his heal but instead is crushed by this mighty man. The Hebrew name for this sign is Akrab which means "the Conflict".

Here we see a **man holding a serpent** that is **trying to steal his crown**!!! As you will see, many of the Zodiac signs are of monsters and beasts. We see this "serpent and monster" theme repeated over and over in the Zodiac. Four of the zodiac signs revolve around beasts and serpents. The serpent (Satan) is presented in many forms but always as an aggressive, venomous and hostile creature.

This is representative of the many battles that God, Jesus and His army of Angels will have to engage in, throughout this age, to suppress the enemy's many attacks (through his many forms) upon God's elect. This sign is also representative of the many struggles and trials that His elect will have to overcome during their journey through life on earth. We too must battle the enemy during our lifetime **to keep the enemy** from **stealing our crown**. God has equipped us to win this battle when we **wear the full armor of God**! And here it is....

Ephesians 6:11-18:

"Put on the whole armor of God that you may be able to stand against the wiles of the devil.
For we do not wrestle against flesh and blood, but against principalities, against powers, against the rulers of the darkness of this age, against spiritual hosts of wickedness in the heavenly places.

*Therefore take up the whole armor of God that you may be
able to withstand in the evil day, and having done all, to stand.
Stand therefore, having girded your waist with truth,
having put on the breastplate of righteousness,
and having shod your feet with the preparation of the gospel
of peace;
above all, taking the shield of faith with which you will be able
to quench all the fiery darts of the wicked one.
And take the helmet of salvation,
and the sword of the Spirit, which is the word of God;
praying always with all prayer and supplication in the Spirit,
being watchful to this end with all perseverance and
supplication for all the saints."*

Serpens - The Struggling Serpent

The first Decan, or minor constellation in the house of Scorpio,
is SERPENS -- the struggling Serpent - as in Satan who
struggles with God and mankind in the battle for man's soul.
Like a serpent he struggles to kill and destroy us both
physically and spiritually

- he tries to steal our life and our crown by possessing
(stealing) our soul.
Serpens is pictured here trying to reach up and steal a strong
man's crown. The strong man is grasping the serpent with
both hands while crushing the scorpion. He most definitely
has the upper hand over the serpent, and demonstrates great
power over the serpent and death!

The Devil is portrayed as a giant serpent in this battle. He is
portrayed in four of the Zodiac signs and in several different
forms; as a serpent; as a dragon; as a scorpion; as Cetus the
water snake; as Leviathan the serpent in the sea; and as
Hydra the many-headed monstrous snake.

This picture depicts the devil as this immense dragon/beast.

The devil has evolved from this tiny serpent in **Genesis 3**, into a great red dragon as described in **Revelation 12:3** because man has given him all of this food (sin) to allow him to grow into the god of this world by our carnal thinking and through our collective minds. He has grown in our minds and thus in our world because mankind has grown in its sinful nature!

During the apocalypse most of mankind will worship Satan and reject God! The earth's exponential population growth has obviously increased Satan's power and influence since he dwells in each of our collective minds - those who are not indwelled with the Holy Spirit of God!

From the first recorded murder when Cain killed his brother Able, mankind has killed an untold number of Christians, Jews, millions of brothers in the battlefields, millions of saints and aborted babies throughout the world. Therefore, billions will die during the Apocalypse, so declares the Lord.

In Rev. Revelation 9:18: we read that 1/3rd of mankind perish from just 3 of seven judgments.

In Revelation 16 one of the angels explains why so much bloodshed is required during the apocalypse:

Revelation 16:4-7:

Then the third angel poured out his bowl on the rivers and springs of water, and they became blood. And I heard the angel of the waters saying:

"You are righteous, O Lord,
The One who is and who was and who is to be,

Because You have judged these things.
For they have shed the blood of saints and prophets,
And You have given them blood to drink.
For it is their just due."

And I heard another from the altar saying, "Even so, Lord
God Almighty, true and righteous is Your judgments."

The serpent that arises **"out of the sea"** (which means: *"out of the nations")* in Revelation, during the apocalypse, *is actually elected into power by mankind* - *who allow him to establish a one world government!* The honor that mankind gives to Antichrist and Satan is the honor that they denied of the creator. In 1 Samuel chapter 8 we see Israel that rejected the Lord's kingship over them, but in the last days it will be **ALL of the nations of the world** that will reject GOD! Let's read....

<u>1 Samuel 8:7-8</u>:

"And the Lord said to Samuel, "Heed the voice of the people in all that they say to you; for they have not rejected you, but they have rejected Me, that I should not reign over them."
"According to all the works which they have done since the day that I brought them up out of Egypt, even to this day—with which they have forsaken Me and served other gods—so they are doing to you also."

So the Antichrist empowered by Satan, comes to power because of the collective spirits of *fallen* mankind who having forsaken the Lord allows this evil beast to supreme power rule the earth in the time of the end!

The carnal mind wants to continue enjoying the pleasures of the flesh and that is one of the hook that Satan will likely use to wield them into his camp of fire and destruction! But fear not, the Lord rules the seas as well **Psalm 93:3-4**.

But those who persevere to the end will be the true victors. The sea of glass in **Revelation 4:16** represents those who live in the earth that have been transformed by the Holy Spirit and are not subject to the roaring seas of the lost, but a sea that is full of peace and serenity because of the word and the spirit of God living inside of them, and the spirit of Jesus who is the **"Prince of Peace"! Love and truth defeats Satan all day long. Rom. 14:17; Jn. 14:27**;

Orphiuchus

The **second Decan** in the house of Scorpio is the picture of a great and powerful man whose name is **Orphiuchus** which means **"the serpent-holder."**

This is a picture of the strong man in a conflict with a great serpent. He is protecting his crown from the claws of the serpent who is desperately trying to steal His crown. What a marvelous portrayal of Jesus Christ Himself whom Satan has been trying since the Garden of Eden to steal His crown! Christ was wounded in the heel when he bled to death at the cross. But upon His resurrection Christ has secured an incorruptible royal crown forevermore, and Satan can never take it away (although he still tries). It is that age long battle between Satan and the seed of the woman **Genesis 3:15**.

The main theme of the bible is about the importance of mankind's soul to both God and Satan. It is truly a life and death struggle for mankind. An age long struggle between good and evil, Christ and Antichrist, the truth and deception, and between eternal life and death.

Hercules

The third and final Decan in the house of Scorpio is HERCULES. He is referred to as the "**god-begotten**" man. Unbeknown to them, even the pagans got this right! The old Hebrew name for Hercules was GIBBOR which has several meanings including: strong man, mighty man, warrior, or champion. This warrior is depicted as being down on one knee. He holds a large club on his right hand. On his left hand he holds a three headed monster called Cerberus. He shoulders the skin of a slain lion. His left foot is positioned directly over the head of the great dragon.

This is clearly another depiction the mighty man **Jesus Christ** who conquers the enemy of this age. Mythical Hercules in reality represents the Lords power and victory over the enemy. Hercules battles all of the beasts referred to in the Zodiac and in mythology, just as Christ has done in reality! Christ stomps the dragon Satan's head in His triumphant final victory against evil. This victory is also promised and transferred to His elect:

Luke 10:19: *"Behold, I give unto you power to tread on serpents and scorpions, and over all the power of the enemy: and nothing shall by any means hurt you".*

Romans 16:20: *"And the God of peace shall bruise Satan under your feet shortly".*

Psalms 91:13: *"Thou shall tread upon the lion and adder, the young lion and the dragon shall you trample under your feet."*

Just like our Lord, **we were designed to subdue Satan (Gen 1:26-28)**! God did not design man to fall prey to Satan, unless man wills it! "In God's image and likeness" means "Perfect" and "all powerful", and capable to resist sin and evil - but again we need to make that choice. God gave us free will -

but if we want to subdue the enemy of this age and his influence in our lives - we need to submit to **_"God's will"_**.

Man's corrupted nature resists being ruled. Because of Adam's choice to eat from the tree of the knowledge of good and evil (Satan), many today think that they are God and that they know enough to survive without God - that is the naked truth that made Adam and Eve realize that they were naked in the Garden. Sin can never be hidden from the Lord! Satan is the master of deception and of evil - He has established his Kingdom on earth - and he lords over it. He is the god of this world and of darkness. He is an evil spirit, and you can see the fruits of his spirit all over our world. Just turn on the morning or evening news and you will witness him hard at work. This is why God must cleanse the world with fire before he can convert earth to heaven. His holy feet cannot touch the filth that permeates this planet at this time of the end. We must decide if we want to be the inhabitants of the earth or the people of God. Remember that Satan is called a thief because he robs us of the truth, our health, our crown and eternal life.

THE MESSAGE of SCORPIO

God is the center of the universe, and that He holds all power through eternity. To worship any other god or idol is to reject God. This is the first of the 10 commandments and a mortal sin which subjects the soul to death. As you have already seen God has no adversary, since he has created everything, and therefore can subdue anything. Satan the serpent, in all of his forms is no threat to sovereign God. He is man's adversary - not God's. His is even powerless over God's Archangel's Michael and Gabriel.

Your reassurance here is that when you choose Jesus as your Lord and savior - Satan has lost his battle for your soul! The blood of the lamb covers and protects your soul from the poisonous darts of the devil! Remember this divine truth, He that is in you (the Holy Spirit) is greater than he that is in the world (Satan and his minions).

Chapter 6 - Sagittarius the Archer

The sun now passes through the constellation Sagittarius - the Archer. This sign is located in the center of our galaxy (Milky Way galaxy). He is a Centaur which is half man and half horse. The man portion is holding a bow and arrow, and is aiming the arrow at the heart of the Scorpion. He is seen riding forth and conquering. In the bible, a horse is associated with war and is a symbol of strength and speed.

The following are several references confirming the association of horses with war and power in the bible:

Isa . 2: 7; 30: 16; Jer. 12: 5; 51: 27; Ezekiel 38: 4 ; Hos. 14: 3; Joel 2: 4; Hag. 2:22; Heb. 1: 8; Amos 4: 10; Isaiah 30:15-16; Rev. 6:2,4,5,8; Rev.19:11; Rev. 19:14; Zech. 10:5;

Jesus is seen in Revelation 19:11-14 riding a white horse with His heavenly army following behind - ready to wage war against all the evil forces on earth at the time of the end:

"Now I saw heaven opened, and behold, a white horse. And He who sat on him was called Faithful and true, and in righteousness He judges and makes war. His eyes were like a flame of fire, and on His head were many crowns. He had a name written that no one knew except Himself. He was clothed with a robe dipped in blood, and His name is called The Word of God. And the armies in heaven, clothed in fine linen, white and clean, followed Him on white horses."

We noted that the Centaur sends the arrow into the heart of the Scorpion - Satan resides in the hearts of fallen mankind. So the man riding the horse (Centaur) is a picture of Jesus the mighty conqueror (the archer), who through the Holy Spirit can remove Satan's influences out of our heart.

This archer is yet another confirmation of who Jesus really is. Christ represents the tree of life in the middle of the Garden of Eden! He who eats of the tree of life (Jesus) will live forever.

Jesus is the bread that came down from heaven! He is symbolic of the manna that sustained the life of the Israelites during their 40 year journey in the desert.

John 6:32:

"Then Jesus said to them, "Most assuredly, I say to you, Moses did not give you the bread from heaven, but My Father gives you the true bread from heaven. For the bread of God is He who comes down from heaven and gives life to the world."

John 6:51:

*"I am the living **bread** which **came down from heaven**. If anyone eats of this **bread, he will live forever;** and the **bread that** I shall give is My flesh, which I shall give for the life of the world."*

Just like this sign is positioned right in the middle of the Milky Way galaxy, it represents Jesus which is representative of the Tree of Life in the middle of the Garden of Eden. This is also a great picture of the Messiah going forth to destroy Satan.

Lyra - the Harp

The first Decan (minor constellation) in the house of Sagittarius is Lyra.
This is an eagle holding a harp. A harp is the symbol of praising the Lord God. This is a picture of how the praise of God through song, music or prayer ascends to heaven and is most pleasing to the Lords ear.

The harp is the only musical instrument mentioned in the book of Revelation; as being used in heaven. So it symbolizes heavenly rejoicing. We read of harps in Rev. 5:8. We see the 24 Elders each having a harp in celebration of the opened scroll giving Jesus title deed to the earth, Again we read of harps in Rev. 14:1-2:

"And I looked and lo, a Lamb stood on the Mount Zion, and with Him an hundred forty and four thousand, having His Father's name written in their foreheads. And I heard a voice from heaven, as the voice of many waters, and as the voice of a great thunder : and I heard the voice of harpers harping with their harps."

King David, a man after the Lord's heart, was also an avid harp player:
I Samuel 16:23: " *And so it was, whenever the spirit from God was upon Saul, that David would take a harp and play it with his hand. Then Saul would become refreshed and well, and the distressing spirit would depart from him.* "

Music will be an important form of worship in paradise as confirmed in the following verses:
Exodus 15; Isaiah 48:20; Isaiah 49:13; Psalm 89:1; Psalm 68:4; Psalm 95; Psalm 101:1; Psalm 147:7; Acts 16:22-25

ARA - The Altar

This second Decan pictures an altar that is in an upside down position - as if pouring fire into the darkness - like into the abyss. Interestingly this constellation is one of the southernmost constellations in the cosmos. Since ancient times this lower region of the heavens was considered representative of the underworld; like Hades or Hell. This sign is one of the consuming fires of judgment that the Messiah

Christ will impose on the serpent (Satan) and all the opposing forces that attack God and His church, throughout the age.
 This altar represents the complete destruction by judgmental fire of all that oppose God and that are associated with the Prince of darkness. God is a consuming fire when he is in judgment mode. The passages below confirm this:

*"For our God is a **consuming fire**."* **Heb. 12:29**
*" Now when the people complained, it displeased the Lord; for the Lord heard it, and His anger was aroused. **So the fire of the Lord burned among them, and consumed some in the outskirts of the camp**."* **Numbers 11:1**
*"When Solomon had finished praying, **fire came down from heaven and consumed the burnt offering** and the sacrifices; and the glory of the Lord filled the temple."* **II Chronicles 7:1**
*"**So fire went out from the Lord and devoured them**, and they died before the Lord."* **Lev. 10:1-2**

And fire appears to be one of the main ways that mankind will be judged during the tribulation period.   Fire is also used to purify and cleanse and it will be necessary to cleanse the world of sin and Satanic control at the time of the end. Zeph. 3:8-9.

"The earth is also defiled under its inhabitants, because they have transgressed the laws, changed the ordinance, broken the everlasting covenant.
Therefore the curse has devoured the earth, and those who dwell in it are held guilty.
Therefore the inhabitants of the earth are burned, *and few men are left."* **Isaiah 24:5**

<u>Draco - the Dragon</u>

This third Decan is a picture of Draco the dragon - none other than Satan.
In Mythology Draco was believed to represent the dragon that fought Minerva during the war between the giants and gods, the dragon at the garden of Hesperides. There are many myths about what Draco represents.

But you and I know better. This is none other than Satan in his symbolic form of a dragon. This is the dragon described in Revelation: 12:3: *"And another sign appeared in heaven: behold, a great, fiery red dragon having seven heads and ten horns, and seven diadems on his heads."*

In **Rev 12:1-3** we read of a great wonder in heaven. A woman (symbolic of Israel) and a red dragon (Satan). Satan has been at war with the nation of Israel from the moment it was founded. As you now know this supernatural battle has been grafted in the heavens? ***Upon careful study of this constellations, we see Draco the dragon (symbolic of Satan) with his eyes fixated upon Virgo (symbolic of the Virgin who will bear the Messiah child), as if it poised to attack and devour her***! Sends chills down my spine!

Chapter 7 - Capricorn the Goat

This constellation depicts a goat with a fish's tail - or a half goat / half fish. This goat appears to be wounded with its head pointing down and knees bent; as if about to die from its wound. It's other half the fish however is lively as if it were full of life.

In the bible, a goat is a sacrificial animal. Jesus is called the Lamb of God that takes away the sins of the world. The message of this sign is that from a dying goat evolves a living fish. The fish has always been a symbol for the church; the body of Christ - the believers.
The fish portion of this sign is clearly a picture of the church or body of Christ which came out of Jesus sacrifice at the cross! Lev. 9:31; Lev. 9:15; Lev. 10:16-17; Mat 4:19; Jer. 16:15-16; Ezekiel 47:1-9; John 3:5.

Among the brightest stars in this marvelous constellation are the following which are appropriately named as follows:

- Al Gedi which means "**the Kid**"
- Deneb Al Gedi which means "**the Sacrifice Cometh**"
- Maasad which means "**the Slaying**"

Sagitta - the Arrow

This first Decan of Capricorn is a picture of an arrow that apparently comes from nowhere - as if from an invisible hand. This is representative of the arrow of God that shoots down from heaven to sacrifice a life to bring forth redemption and new life. Jesus was the sacrificial lamb that this arrow pierced for the redemption of sin, so that out of His sacrifice, millions could receive eternal LIFE.

Psalm 38:2 *"For Your arrows pierce me deeply, And Your hand presses me down."*
Isaiah 53:4 *"Surely He has borne our grief and carried our sorrows; yet we esteemed Him stricken, smitten by God, and afflicted.*
Job 6:4 *"For the arrows of the Almighty are within me; My spirit drinks in their poison; the terrors of God are arrayed against me."*

Aquila

The second Decan is called Aquila which pictures a pierced eagle. An eagle is considered to be the highest form of bird - the king of the birds if you will. Biblically, it is a symbol of the upward flight in the quest to re-unite with the creator in heaven. Throughout the bible, the Eagle is referenced as a symbol of divinity.

*'You have seen what I did to the Egyptians, and how **I bore you on eagles' wings** and brought you to Myself."* **Exodus 19:4**

Other References: Deut. 32:11; Deut. 28:49; Psalm 103:5; Rev. 4:7; Prov.30:18-19; Job 39:29;

This pierced eagle is representative of Christ who was pierced for our sins. The church is also symbolic of the eagle, in that it will also ascend to heaven at the resurrection of the saints.

Delphinus

The third Decan of Capricorn is the picture of a Dolphin that leaps out of the water. Water here is symbolic with death. So this dolphin shoots up out of death as in the resurrection of the Lord on the third day after His death!

Chapter 8 - Aquarius the Water Pourer

We now enter the sign of Aquarius referred to as "Water Pourer". This is the picture of a mighty person holding a great urn over his shoulders. Out of the urn pours an endless stream of water into the mouths of a large fish.

Water is also a symbol of the Holy Spirit since it cleanses the body of its sinful nature. Aquarius is a symbol of God's pouring out of the Holy Spirit upon His elect. So this symbol represents the body of Christ and the fullness of the Lord. This picture represents the Lord's promise to pour out His Holy Spirit for all who thirst and call out His name. One can also interpret this as an outpouring of the word of God which also nourished the mind and soul.

As we already know Christ is the word, which has existed since the beginning (John 1: 1. Jesus Christ is representative of that large fish, the firstborn of many fish, whom God poured the full measure of His spirit upon. Jesus then became a vessel of the Holy Spirit for whoever calls on Him and accepts His blood and body as their hope for redemption.
So the age of Aquarius is not indicative of more of the same, but rather a new age whereby God will make a new heaven and new earth out of this sinful age.

The southern Fish

The first Decan of Aquarius is a large fish as already discussed. It is called "The Southern Fish". It consists of one bright star which is named "Fomalhaut" or the "mouth of the fish". This sign was already identified as the large fish that receives the water from the "mighty man" and identified it as all who drink of the ever-flowing living water that is poured out from the Lord for all who thirst for the word and the Holy Spirit.

John 7:37 clearly relays the meaning of this sign: *"On the last day, that great day of the feast, Jesus stood and cried out, saying, "If anyone thirsts, let him come to Me and drink."*

Pegasus - The Winged Horse

The second Decan in the house of Aquarius is Pegasus - the winged horse. This constellation hosts 89 stars. Among the brightest stars are:
- Markab - which means **"returning from afar"**
- Scheat - which means **"who goes and returns"**
- Enif - which means **"the branch"**
- Al Genib - which means **"who carries"**
- Matar - which means **"who causes the plenteous overflow"**

From this and in relationship with the other signs of Aquarius we can determine that this sign is of one who is returning from far away. He is the branch. He bears much water that causes an abundant overflow. Jesus is the branch and from Him flows rivers of living water:

John 7:38: *"He who believes in Me, as the Scripture has said, out of his heart will flow rivers of living water."*

Revelation 7:17: "for the Lamb who is in the midst of the throne will shepherd them and lead them to **living** fountains of **water**s. And God will wipe away every tear from their eyes."

The Swan

Now we explore the 3rd Decan of Aquarius referred to as the Swan. The swan is a very beautiful and majestic bird that flies over water. This swan which also appears to be in the form of a cross becomes a dual image of a swan bearing the cross. This swan-cross is pictured as flying through the heavens with great speed. It is on the same path as the river of endless living water (symbol of Holy Spirit) that flows from the heavenly urn. This is a symbol of a swan carrying the cross reflecting that Christ's death at the cross, the release of the Holy Spirit became manifest. This sign brings home the message that only through Christ's sacrifice at the cross, could the Holy Spirit be released.

"This spoke Jesus of the Spirit, which they that believed on Him were to receive; for the Spirit was not yet given; because Jesus was not yet glorified" **(Jn. 7: 39)**.
 "as many as are led by the Spirit of God, they are the sons of God" **(Rom. 8: 14)**.

Chapter 9 - PISCES the Fishes

As we continue on our journey through the heavens, we now see the sun pass through the constellation Pisces - the fishes. Here we have a picture of two fishes. One fish is swimming northward, and the other fish is swimming in a straight line horizontally - towards the sun. The two fishes are connected by the tail by a band which is also attached to the neck of a sea monster (Cetus).

This sign is located directly below Andromeda (Chained Woman), and above Andromeda is Cepheus, a bearded King sitting on a throne, wearing a crown and royal attire, and holding a scepter. A lot of activity here! In his position in the sky he is a picture of the liberator of the chained woman.

The two fishes are clearly a representation of the church. This connection between fish and the body of Christ is sprinkled throughout the gospels. The sea represents the lowest depths of civilization where sin and death abide. So casting the fish out of the sea is representative of being born again, and rescued out of the sea of depravity. Here are just a few examples:

*"I will send for many fishers, and they shall fish them"
(Jer. 16: 15-16).*
*"And there shall be a very great multitude of fish,
because the waters shall come thither" (Ezekiel 47: 1-9).*

*"The wicked are like the troubles sea, which cannot rest,
whose waters cast up mire and dirt. There is no peace,
says my God, to the wicked" (Isaiah 57: 20-21).*

"Follow Me, and I will make you fishers of men" (Mat. 4: 19).

Jesus answered, "Most assuredly, I say to you, unless one is born of water and the Spirit, he cannot enter the kingdom of God. (John 3:5)

"These are RAGING WAVES OF THE SEA, foaming out their own shame" (Jude 13)
"The waters which thou saw, where the whore sits, are peoples, and multitudes, and tongues" (Revelation 17: 15).

As indicated, these two fishes are connected, inseparably tied together, by a band and are headed in the same direction, but one is pointing to the heavens and the other horizontally towards the sun.

The fish headed upwards represents the coming reward and heavenly home that awaits the body of Christ. The fish swimming horizontally toward the sun represent the body of Christ on earth persevering in their journey through life focused on and leading others to the Son of God; the light of the world.

The Band

The first Decan, or minor constellation, in the House of Pisces is called **"The Band"**.
This band binds the fishes, being fastened around the tails of the two fishes so that these two are as one. The picture here is that once we receive the Holy Spirit and are following the light we become one with Christ and no force can separate that bond.

We also observe that the band is also attached to the neck of the dragon (in the form of Cetus the sea monster). The later represents the ongoing persecution and bondage from Satan towards the body of Christ - Church. Notwithstanding however, we also see Aries the Lamb with his paw on the

band restraining the spiritual attacks of the beast upon the Church - another example that Christ is in control and will never allow Satan from destroying His church. In the **book of Isaiah, the prophet speaks of the band, and how the chains that bind the woman will be loosed at the appointed time…**

Isaiah 52:1-3

Awake, awake!
Put on your strength, O Zion;
Put on your beautiful garments,
O Jerusalem, the holy city!
For the uncircumcised and the unclean
Shall no longer come to you.
Shake yourself from the dust, arise;
Sit down, O Jerusalem! Loosen yourself from the bonds
of your neck,
O captive daughter of Zion!

Andromeda - the chained woman

The second Decan in the House of Pisces is a sign of a woman with her arms and feet chained. She is suffering under bondage, affliction and persecution. In the bible, the woman is a symbol of the church, the bride of Christ. Andromeda is the picture of the body of Christ!

Although the church is seen afflicted in this picture it is because this is church in its present state, before it is transformed into the bride of Christ in heaven.

Ephesians 5:27: *that He might present her to Himself a glorious church, not having spot or wrinkle or any such thing, but that she should be holy and without blemish.*

II Corinthians 11:2: *For I am jealous for you with godly jealousy. For I have betrothed you to one husband, that I may present you as a chaste virgin to Christ.*

Revelation 21:9-11: *Then one of the seven angels who had the seven bowls filled with the seven last plagues came to me and talked with me, saying, "Come, I will show you the bride, the Lamb's wife." And he carried me away in the Spirit to a great and high mountain, and showed me the great city, the holy Jerusalem, descending out of heaven from God, having the glory of God. Her light was like a most precious stone, like a jasper stone, clear as crystal.*

Cepheus - The King

We now journey to the third Decan in the house of Pisces; Cepheus - the king. Cepheus in Hebrew means "Royal Branch". The Ethiopians called this sign Hyk which means "The King".

This is the picture of a great king, positioned in the highest part of the cosmos. He is the king who delivers the chained woman in bondage (Andromeda - the 3nd Decan). He holds a scepter on his raised hand. The ancient Egyptians referred to this constellation as Pekuhor, which means "The Ruler That Comes".

Among the most stars in this group are:
- Alphirk, which means **"The Redeemer"**
- Al Deramin, which means **"Coming Quickly"**

Without doubt this sign is referring to **the Lord of hosts.**

Chapter 10 - ARIES the Lamb

The Sun now continues its yearly trek passing through the zodiac sign **Aries - the Lamb.**
Although it has more recently been portrayed as a Ram, the oldest record on the Zodiac portrays Aries as a lamb. This lamb has no horns. It is like the type of lamb that would be sacrificed - a perfect lamb without blemish. Aries Hebrew name is Taleh which translates to "The Lamb Sent Forth". The Greek translation for Krios is "the Lamb". The Latin translation is easy because the constellation is called Aries in Latin also meaning "the Lamb". The names of the stars in this group help determine the meaning of this sign. The Arabic term for Aries is Hamal which means sheep, gentle.

The brightest stars in the group have the following names/meaning:

- ELNATH which means "the Slain"
- SHERETAN, which means "Bruised"
- MESARTIM, which means "The Bound"

The above is a clear picture of the Lamb of God that takes away the sins of the world.
While in the Old Testament before the Messiah, atonement for sin required an animal sacrifice - such as a lamb or ram. But Jesus would make the animal sacrifices obsolete, through His blood at the cross - the perfect sacrifice that covers the sins of the world.
"Behold the Lamb of God, which takes away the sin of the world" (John. 1: 29)

"For God so loved the world, that He gave His only begotten Son..." (Jn. 3: 16)
"Upon Him that loved us, and washed us from our sins in His own blood" (Rev. 1: 5).

"Worthy is the Lamb that was slain to receive power, and riches, and wisdom, and strength, and honor, and glory, and blessing..." (Rev. 5: 12)

"And they overcame him by the blood of the Lamb" (Rev. 12: 11)

"the LAMB slain from the foundation of the world" (Rev. 13: 8)

"a LAMB without blemish or spot... foreordained before the foundation of the world" (1 Pet. 1: 19-20).

Cassiopeia - The Enthroned Woman

Among the Decans of Aries is called Cassiopeia - which means **"The Enthroned Woman"**. This is a picture of a queen; very beautiful, seated as on a throne high up in the heavens. She holds the branch of victory on one hand and in the other she seems to be arranging herself as if ***preparing herself for a ceremonious event***. Near her sits the King Cepheus in an adjacent throne. A clear representation here is that this is the bride of Christ (the church), prepared for the marriage supper of the Lamb.

"Let us be glad and rejoice, and give honor to Him, for the marriage of the Lamb is come, and His wife hath made herself ready" (Rev. 19:7)

"And I John saw the Holy City, New Jerusalem, coming down from God out of heaven, prepared as a bride adorned for her husband" (Rev. 21: 2)
"Behold, THE TABERNACLE OF GOD IS WITH MEN, and He will dwell with them, and they shall be His people, and God Himself shall be with them and be their God" (Rev. 21: 3)

Chapter 11 - Taurus the Bull

As the Sun passes through the Cosmos it now enters the zodiac star group called Taurus, which means "**the Bull**". This is a picture of a bull charging with his head lowered and ready to attack. Yet this bull seems to have grown out of Aries - the lamb. So it is like the Lamb of Aries that is now transformed into a bull.

Located in the eye of the bull is the main star in Taurus named Al Debaran, which means "the Governor".

This grand constellation is a picture of Christ the sacrificial Lamb changing roles as he returns to enact judgment upon Satan, the flesh, and the fallen world. This represents the dual nature of the Lamb of God - **Christ is both the SAVIOUR and the JUDGE of the universe.**

There is no doubt that the sign of Taurus is one of judgment, and the going forward of Christ to enact judgment. This coming judgment is referred to as the "wrath of the Lamb" in the book of Revelation.

Revelation 6:16:

*"And the kings of the earth, the great men, the rich men, the commanders, the mighty men, every slave and every free man, hid themselves in the caves and in the rocks of the mountains, and said to the mountains and rocks, "Fall on us and hide us from the face of **Him who sits on the throne** and from the **wrath of the Lamb**!*

The following verses explain some of the who and the why of the coming judgment upon the world:
"The Lord Jesus shall be revealed from heaven with His mighty angels, in flaming fire taking vengeance on them

that know not God, and that obey not the gospel of our Lord Jesus Christ" (II Thes. 1: 7-8)

"For He is coming, He is coming to judge the earth. He shall judge the world with righteousness and the peoples with His truth." (Psalm 96:13)

"For it is the day of the Lord's vengeance, the year of recompense for the cause of Zion." (Isaiah 34:8).

"The Lord Jesus shall be revealed from heaven with His mighty angels, in flaming fire taking vengeance on them that know not God, and that obey not the gospel of our Lord Jesus Christ" (II Thes. 1: 7-8).

"God is preparing a mighty company of judges whose responsibility it shall be to judge the world in righteousness!" Daniel 7: 21-22

"To him will I give power over the nations: and he shall rule them with a rod of iron" (Rev. 2: 26-27). *"And I saw thrones, and they sat on them, and judgment was given unto them"* (Rev. 20: 4,6).

"Do ye not know that the saints shall judge the world? And if the world shall be judged by you, are ye unworthy to judge the smallest matters? Know ye not that we shall judge angels? How much more things that pertain to this life" (I Cor. 6: 2-3).

Orion - The Great Hunter

The first of the minor constellations (Decan) of Taurus is Orion. Orion means, "coming forth in Light". Orion is the picture of a great hunter. He has a large club raised high in his right hand. In his left hand is the skin of a lion (marked with small stars) which he has killed. He wears a sword on his belt, and there is a small triangle shaped on his head. The hilt of the sword is in the shape of a lamb.

This constellation appears in the following scriptures:

Job 9:9 " He made the Bear, Orion, and the Pleiades, and the chambers of the south;"
Job: 38:31: "Can you bind the cluster of the Pleiades, or loosen the belt of Orion?'
Amos 5:8: " He made the Pleiades and Orion; He turns the shadow of death into morning and makes the day dark as night; He calls for the waters of the sea and pours them out on the face of the earth; the Lord *is* His name."
The Hebrew name for Orion is "**a Strong One; a Hero**".
The Egyptian name means "**This is He Who Triumphs**".

Orion is one of - if not the most magnificent of all the constellations in the cosmos.

It is so brilliantly beautiful to behold, that words cannot adequately describe it. It is like a giant diamond in the sky illumined from within and studded with millions of stars, extending for trillions of miles through space. It most definitely declares the Glory of God. The ancients tried to glorify their heroes, kings and mythological figures by comparing them to Orion.   But that honor belongs to its creator. Orion is a picture of none other than the Lord in all His glory in heaven. It also depicts the body of Christ resurrected in all its glory.

"Like the appearance of a rainbow in a cloud on a rainy day, so was the appearance of the brightness all around it. This was the appearance of the likeness of the glory of the Lord." **Ezekiel 1:28**

Indeed, the union of the seven stars into the one body of Christ is depicted in the heavens as Great Orion. In the fullness of time, the Lord will 'loose the bands of Orion,' and

62

the manifestation of the sons of God will take place. "In His discussions with Job, the Lord asked him where he was when He laid the foundations of the world, and also, 'when the **morning stars sang together**, and all the sons of God shouted for joy:

 "Where were you when I laid the foundations of the earth?
Tell Me, if you have understanding.
Who determined its measurements?
Surely you know!
Or who stretched the line upon it?
To what were its foundations fastened?
Or who laid its cornerstone,
When the morning stars sang together,
And all the sons of God shouted for joy? (Job 38: 4-7).
"The mystery of the seven stars which thou saw in My right hand, and the seven golden candlesticks. The seven stars are the angels (messengers) of the seven churches: and the seven candlesticks which thou saw are the seven churches." (Rev. 1: 20).

Eradanus

The second Decan in the house of Taurus is Eradanus which means "the River of the Judge". It is a picture of a molten river (like a glowing lava flow) which flows out from Orion. It runs through Cetus the Sea-monster and disappears into the dark recesses of space. This is a sign of a great judgment with fire. The Lord's tongue is like a devouring fire (Isaiah 30:27)

Here are some bible verses which speak of the coming judgment fire:

*"He himself shall also drink of the wine of the wrath of God, which is poured out full strength into the cup of His indignation. **He shall be tormented with fire and brimstone***

in the presence of the holy angels and in the presence of the Lamb." (Rev. 14:10)

*"But the cowardly, unbelieving, abominable, murderers, sexually immoral, sorcerers, idolaters, and all liars **shall have their part in the lake which burns with fire and brimstone, which is the second death."** (Rev. 21:8)*

*"Our God shall come, and shall not keep silence: **a fire shall devour before Him, and it shall be very tempestuous round about Him"** (Ps. 50: 3)*

Auriga

The third (or minor constellation) of Taurus is "Auriga - the great shepherd. Auriga is a Hebrew word for **"a Shepherd"**. We already discussed the great Bull Taurus, and the fire of judgment displayed by the constellation Eridanus. Auriga is seated, holding a female goat on his left shoulder. The goat's paws wrap around the neck of Auriga in fear of the raging bull. He holds two trembling baby goats on his lap.

This is a clear picture of our Lord who protects and carries His flock like the great Shepherd that He is; protecting us from all the fiery darts of the enemy. Here are a few related bible verses:

*"Behold, the Lord God will come with a strong hand, and His arm shall rule for Him: behold, His reward is with Him, and His work before Him. He shall feed His flock like a shepherd: **He shall gather the lambs with His arm, and carry them in His bosom, and shall gently lead those that are with young"** (Isa. 40: 10-11).*

There is a very bright star in the foot of Auriga called **El Nath**, which means **"wounded or slain"**. This clearly identifies Auriga as a picture of Jesus, the good shepherd, who was wounded in the heal by the serpent - nearly 2,000 years ago at the cross. This was foretold in Genesis 3:15 by God Himself (Gods Great prophecy), whereby God tells Satan that he will wound and bruise His lamb Jesus at the cross, but Jesus will return to crush his head!

"And I will put enmity between you and the woman, and between your seed and her Seed; He shall bruise your head, and you shall bruise His heel." (Genesis 3:15)

<u>Here is scriptural evidence that Jesus is the Good Shepherd</u>:

"I am the good shepherd. The good shepherd gives His life for the sheep." (John 10:11)

"and when the Chief Shepherd appears, you will receive the crown of glory that does not fade away." (1 Peter 5:4)

"He that enters in by the door is the shepherd of the sheep. And he calls his own sheep by name, and leads them out" (John. 10:2-3)

"What man of you, having a hundred sheep, if he loses one of them, does not leave the ninety-nine in the wilderness, and go after the one which is lost until he finds it?" (Luke 15:4)

<u>Additional Related Verses on Jesus - the great Shepherd:</u>

Psalm 23; John 10:2-3-6; Heb. 13:20-21; Jn. 5:24-26; Heb. 4:7; John 5:24-26; John 1:1-10; Acts 3:22; 1 Thes. 4:15, 17; Ps. 24:1; Isa. 53:6; Isa. 55:6-7; I Pet. 2:25; Luke 15:4; Eph. 1:10 John 10:11-14; 10:39

Chapter 12 - Gemini the Twins

The sun now makes its way through the tenth Zodiac sign (Constellation) referred to as Gemini - the Twins. Here is a picture of 2 young twins, in a restful position with their heads rested against each other. The one on the left has a club in his hand but even the club is in a rested position. The one on the right has a harp in one hand and a bow and arrow in the other (again in a rested position). They are resting, but they are at the ready for anything that may come their way. They portray great confidence perhaps due to prior victories and expectations for ultimate victory.

The Hebrew name for Gemini is Thaumim which means **"united and joined together".**
While Greek mythology wants you to think that these twins stand for the heroes Hercules and Apollo, their Latin names are Castor and Pollux, named after the two bright stars in the heads of each of these twins.

The twins are also a picture of the law of polarity which requires perfect balance in the universe and in the character of the creator. All creation operates in a state of balance. Electricity operates on negative and positive polarity.

Here are some other samples of polarity as related to the natural and the supernatural:
- Wrath and Mercy
- Life and Death
- Good and evil
- Light and darkness
- Positive and Negative magnetic polarization

So is the case on how the creator operates in the natural and supernatural realm:

- There had to be evil in order for there to be good.

- God must right the wrong, in order to maintain balance and unity.
- God's left hand corrects sin, while His right hand blesses and redeems.
- Our mind also is created with free will - se we have a left mind which represents our sinful nature - the carnal side of our thinking; and a right mind which represents true love and the traits of God's Holy Spirit.
- There are two sides to divine love: *"for whom the Lord loves He chastens, and scourges every son whom He receives"* (**Heb. 12: 6**).
- The Old Testament reveals God's left hand of discipline, while the New Testament reveals God's right hand of mercy, grace love and redemption. His right hand is stronger than His left hand. His left hand is called the **"hidden hand"**. This is because God who is patient and Love shows much more mercy than judgment.

" Therefore being exalted to the <u>right hand of God</u>, and having received from the Father the promise of the Holy Spirit, He poured out this which you now see and hear." **Acts 2:33**

"who has gone into heaven and is at the right hand of God, angels and authorities and powers having been made subject to Him." **1 Peter 3:22**

<u>**Related verses**</u>:

Mathew 25:31-46; Rev 1:16-20; Mat. 28:18; Col. 3:1; Psalm 89:25; Eze. 47:1-9; Dan. 7:27-28; Isaiah 55:8-1

Note that the right hand of God represents His authority, power, dominion, and wisdom. His right hand represents His fullness - God's omnipotence.
Jesus is seated at the right hand of God, thus ALL authority and power is bestowed upon Christ.

The body of Christ (His church) will also be seated at the right hand of the father in heaven representing God's government in the Kingdom of God.

The right hand of God is the anointed hand. Christ is the anointed and He sits at the right hand of the Father. The word Christ means "The Anointed"!

Reigning with Christ and sitting on His right hand, should become the number one goal of every living soul. On earth it seems like most everybody wants to have power, and those few that don't admire those with power. How sad that so few are aware of the "REAL" power, the supernatural kingdom power, that they can attain through perpetuity by placing their trust and life in Jesus hands! Paul tells us something about it in Eph . 1: 16-23.

Here are some powerful and exciting verses confirming the above and our future role in heaven:

"To him who overcomes I will grant to sit with Me on My throne, as I also overcame and sat down with My Father on His throne." **Rev. 3:21**

" And Jesus came and spoke to them, saying, "All authority has been given to Me in heaven and on earth." **Mathew 28:18**

"and raised us up together, and made us sit together in the heavenly places in Christ Jesus," **Ephesians 2:6**

"And He put all things under His feet, and gave Him to be head over all things to the church, which is His body, the fullness of Him who fills all in all." **Ephesians 1:22-23**

Canis Minor

This is the first Decan of Gemini and is referred to as Canis Minor, which means "the lesser Dog". Despite its name, the ancients referred to the figure as a hawk's head and it was called Sebak.

Its brightest star is called Procyon which means "the redeemer"
Since Canis Minor and Canis Major are interconnected, the meaning of this sign will continue with the following Decan - Canis Major.

Canis Major

This second Decan is referred to as Canis Major which means "the greater Dog". Again as with Canis Minor, the ancients depicted this constellation as a Hawk. Canis Major hosts the brightest star in the Cosmos which is called Sirius, meaning "*Prince*".

Also, the ancient Zodiac called Canis Major **"Apes"**, which means **"the head",** and it was pictured as a human with the head of a hawk. A hawk is the natural enemy of the serpent (snake).

The name Canis Major's host star is Naz, which means **"caused to come forth"**.
Among His many names, Jesus is referred to as a **"Prince"** in the bible:

"For unto us a Child is born, unto us a Son is given; and the government will be upon His shoulder. And His name will be called Wonderful, Counselor, Mighty God, Everlasting Father, Prince of Peace." **Isaiah 9:6**

So these two hawk figures are a very similar sign as that of its major constellation Gemini. These are both twins, and they depict the dual role of Messiah Jesus as the "**Prince of Peace**" who came to offer us redemption for our sins, and "the **Prince that is to come**" to destroy the serpent once and for all!

Chapter 13 - Cancer the Crab

The sun now passes through the eleventh of twelve signs of the Zodiac called "Cancer" - the Crab. The name **Cancer** comes from a Latin root meaning **"To hold or encircle"**. The Greek interpretation is pretty much the same. This image of a crab is thus used because of the crab's ability to hold onto something very firmly with its relatively large claws. How sad that a horrible disease, that inflicts so much suffering on mankind shares the same name as such a glorious star group with such a wonderful and joyful message as the constellation Cancer reveals.

In the middle of the Sign of Cancer is one of the most brilliant nebulous in all of the cosmos. This cluster of stars is called **Praesepe**, which stands for "***the Multitude***".
All Crabs, even those that can live on land, return to the sea to breed. They are born of the water. Like the Crab, the church is born of water and of the Holy Spirit - which is symbolized as water. And as the crab can live in two environments (land and water), the church also resides in two environments; earth and heaven. Our body belongs on earth but our spirit belongs in heaven. Of course it is not a free trip; to make it to heaven our mind must be transformed. With the help of the Holy Spirit we can transform our mind from carnally minded to spiritually minded.

"And do not be conformed to this world, but be transformed by the renewing of your mind, that you may prove what is that good and acceptable and perfect will of God." (Romans 12:2)

"For our citizenship is in heaven, from which we also eagerly wait for the Savior, the Lord Jesus Christ, [21] who will transform our lowly body that it may be conformed to His glorious body, according to the working by which He

is able even to subdue all things to Himself." (Phil. 3:20-21)

"For to be carnally minded is death, but to be spiritually minded is life and peace." (Romans 8:6)

So this is clearly a picture of the church, the seed of Abraham, and Christ. It is displayed as a vast heavenly "multitude", innumerable like the sand on the beach, and the stars in the heavens.

From Abraham's seed came Jesus, whereby all the families of the earth would become blessed. So Jesus had to sacrifice His life for the redemption; that would manifest the seed of Christ, His church. All who are from the seed of Jesus Christ (those who accept Christ as Lord and savior) are de facto Abraham's seed, regardless of their race or origin. Read the passages below:

"There is neither Jew nor Greek, neither slave nor free, neither male nor female; for you are all one in Christ Jesus. And if you are Christ's, then you are Abraham's seed, and heirs according to the promise." (Galatians 3:28-29)

"Now to Abraham and his Seed were the promises made. He does not say, "And to seeds," as of many, but as of one, "And to your Seed," who is Christ." Galatians 3:16

"The hour is come that the Son of man should be glorified. Verily , verily, I say unto you, Except a corn of wheat fall into the ground and die, it abides alone: but if it dies, it brings forth much fruit" (John. 12: 23-24).

Ursa Minor - the Little Fold (Lesser Bear)

The first Decan in the house of Cancer is **Ursa Minor**, has lately been referred to as the Lesser Bear; however it was originally called "***Little Fold***" - which should be the correct sign. As you will soon discover my brothers and sisters - ***there is nothing minor about Ursa Minor***!

Important Note: The ancients did ***NOT*** refer to this constellation as a bear, as it does not even have the characteristics of a bear; as this image has a very long tail. There are no traces of a bear in the original Zodiacs of Chaldea, Egypt, India or even Persia. It was the ***Ancient Greeks***, in their obsession with mythical heroes and idols which changed the interpretation to that of a bear. **The original meaning for this Decan, however was that of a "*little fold*"**. Ursa Minor is a representation of the manifested children of God.

Ursa Minor hosts what is considered to be ***the most significant star in all of the heavens.*** It is also the major star of this star group. Its original name is ***Al-Ruccaba***, which means **"ridden on".** The name today is **"Polaris"** or **"*the North Star*".** ***This appears to be the central star of the universe since all other heavenly bodies appear to revolve around it.*** It does not appear to move in a circular fashion as all the other stars! ***This star is representative of none other than our Messiah by whom all things, just like the North Star, are under His feet.***

*"And He put all things **under His feet**, and gave Him to be head over all things to the church, which is His body, the fullness of Him who fills all in all."* **Ephesians 1:22-23**
IMPORTANT NOTE: In ancient times (approx. 6,000 years ago) when the constellations were first mapped, the Pole Star was ***not Polaris***, but rather, it was the star ***Draconis***, the main star in the constellation of ***Draco the Dragon***!

This fact is divinely significant! At that time, the dragon, the serpent, which is Satan the devil in all of his forms, deceived mankind at the Garden of Eden and became the god of this earth, he stole the lordship over the earth right from ___under man's feet___!

And mankind fell from grace. They were hence expelled from the Garden of Eden, which was heaven on earth. Around that time Draconis (the dragon) became the North Star (Pole Star), upon which all the heavenly bodies seem to revolve around. *Now get ready for the good part*!

So at one time the Dragon seemed to have a position of godhead over the earth which was confirmed by the North Star. However, with the gradual movement of the equinoxes, that position of honor changed. *Draconis* has now moved quite a distance from the Pole, and has **NOW** been replaced by the star of glory - *Polaris* - the King star of the constellation Ursa Minor; the little fold - ___the star that represents the children of God Almighty!___

Everything in heaven now revolves around the King star; the star that represents our Messiah Christ! All the heavens revolve around His name, to declare to all mankind that Jesus Christ is not dead - He is alive, and He will soon return to recapture what is His!
What Satan wants to hide from mankind with mythical misrepresentations of the truths recorded in the Zodiac; the heavens clearly disclose for all who yearn for the TRUTH!

Behold, God's message to Satan was declared from the very beginning of mankind. And it is: ___"Satan, you may have won the battle, but you will NOT win the war!"___

*"And I will put enmity between you (Satan) and the woman, and between your seed and her Seed; **He (Messiah) shall***

bruise your head, *and you shall bruise His heel."* **Genesis 3:15**

Jesus will soon return in all His Glory to reclaim what was stolen from mankind:

"Now I saw heaven opened, and behold, a white horse. And He who sat on him was called Faithful and True, and in righteousness He judges and makes war. His eyes were like a flame of fire, and on His head were **many crowns**. *He had a name written that no one knew except Himself. He was clothed with* **a robe dipped in blood**, *and His name is called* **The Word of God**. *And the armies in heaven, clothed in fine linen, white and*

clean, followed Him on white horses. Now out of His mouth goes a sharp sword, that with it He should strike the nations. And He Himself will rule them with a rod of iron. He Himself treads the winepress of the fierceness and wrath of Almighty God. And He has on His robe and on His thigh a name written: **KING OF KINGS AND LORD OF LORDS."**
Revelation 19:11-16

Ursa Major - the Great Fold

The second Decan in the house of Cancer is **Ursa Major** and as is the case with Ursa Minor, the original and correct meaning of this Decan is "**great fold**". Whereas Ursa Minor represents the children of God, I believe that Ursa Major represents the manifest body of Christ; His church in all of its Glory in heaven. My brothers and sisters, we have no idea what Glory awaits us in paradise:

"(The) eye has not seen, nor ear heard, neither has entered the heart of man, the things which God has

prepared for them that love Him." (I Cor. 2: 9)

"For I reckon that the sufferings of this present time are not worthy to be compared with the glory that shall be revealed in us." (Romans 8:18)

Argo - The Ship

The 3rd Decan (minor constellation), in this marvelous house of Cancer is **Argo**, which means "**the Ship**".

It is a picture of a large ship with its sails rolled up indicating that it has completed its journey and returned home to its harbor. When we consider the meanings of Cancer and the other two Decans in its house, it becomes clear that this ship represents Christ who has delivered His bride (the Church) safely home to its harbor. Its harbor represents God's heavenly abode. The only way to the God of Abraham, Isaac and Jacob is through His ship, Messiah Jesus - just as Jesus declared:

"I am the way, the truth, and the life: no man comes unto the Father but by Me" (Jn. 14: 6).

Chapter 14 - LEO the LION

The sun now reaches its final destination for the year as it passes through the twelfth and final Zodiac sign named **Leo the Lion**. We have now gone full circle - witnessed by the tail of the lion which points to the head of Virgo. Even the great Sphinx of Egypt unknowingly acknowledges this momentous sign, with the head of a woman and the tail of a Lion!

The name of this final sign, **Leo the Lion**, has been accepted by all of the ancient civilizations, and it means "**He that Tears Asunder**". The lion is the King of all animals, capable of crushing the bones of just about any other beast. *__When the Lord Jesus returns as the Lion of the Tribe of Judah - He will crush all of the bones in the head of the beast - Satan.__* And Messiah alone will reign forevermore as the King of Kings and the Lord of Lords - **End of story**!

This 12th and final sign in the heavens fits perfectly with the final chapter of the bible! In fact the first and last sign of the Zodiac coincide perfectly with the first and last books of the bible. Is this why Jesus declares that He is the *first and the last*?

So we started this journey with Virgo (the seed of the woman), and conclude with Leo the Lion (The Lion of the Tribe of Judah)! The woman is introduced in the first book of the bible with God's great prophecy (**Genesis 3:15**); and then the Lion of the Tribe of Judah is introduced in heaven - in the last book of the bible:

"Weep not: behold, the Lion of the tribe of Judah, the Root of David, has prevailed to open the book, and to loosen the seven seals thereof" (Revelation 5: 5).

We have already read the outcome of the Cosmic battle between good and evil as foretold in many of the Zodiac signs and their Decans including Scorpio, Taurus, Setus, and Orion. *Ah how the best has been saved for last!* Just like the end of our journey marks the beginning of everlasting Joy and peace, the last of the Zodiac signs represents the beginning of a new age - featuring a *New heaven and a New Earth*! Just like the finale of the classic movies and storylines of old - **in the end *the good side always wins*!** And that is the core of the message behind **Leo the Lion**!

Hydra - the Serpent

The first Decan of the constellation Leo the Lion is Hydra - the Great Serpent. Hydra stands for "***the Abhorred***". Hydra is the sign of a great snake (serpent) that spans 100 degrees across the heavens. Situated below Cancer, Leo, and Virgo, Hydra is a picture of Satan whom has reached the end of his rope in that his head stands beneath the foot of Leo. Leo the lion appears to be pouncing the head of the serpent in a show of final victory against that serpent of old; thus fulfilling God's first great prophecy in Genesis:

*"And I will put enmity between thee and the woman, and between thy seed and her seed; **it shall bruise thy head**, and thou shall bruise his heel"* **(Genesis 3:15)**

Christ is pictured crushing the head of the dragon/serpent in 4 of the 12 constellations. God wants to make it clear to us that it makes no sense to follow in the path of the serpent by living in sin; as it will lead us also to destruction. Why should we allow Satan to crush our head, when the Lion of the Tribe of Judah has already crushed his head; having already won that battle for us!

Crater - The Cup

The second Decan of Leo the Lion is **Crater the cup**. It is a very small constellation that packs a big punch! Crater is situated below the hind feet of Leo and rests on the serpent Hydra. Part of this star group is inside the house of the serpent; a sign of unambiguous contact. Crater is not the cup of joy that the ancient Greeks believed, but rather it is the cup of the wrath of God; of His indignation, and the cup of the fierceness of His wrath as foretold in the following passages:

"he himself shall also drink of the wine of the wrath of God, which is poured out full strength into the cup of His indignation. He shall be tormented with fire and brimstone in the presence of the holy angels and in the presence of the Lamb."
Revelation 14:10

"Now the great city was divided into three parts, and the cities of the nations fell. And great Babylon was remembered before God, to give her the cup of the wine of the fierceness of His wrath." **Rev. 16:19**

<u>Related Verses</u>: **Psalm 75:8; Psalm 11:6; Rev. 18:4-6; Rev. 12:1; Rev. 14:4;**

<u>Corvus - The Raven</u>

We now enter the third and last Decan in the last sign of the Zodiac Leo the Lion! Its name is Corvus - the Raven. The raven is a scavenger bird with a powerful three inch beak designed to tear away the flesh of dead animals. The Raven is pictured here grasping the body of Hydra the serpent and tearing up his flesh with his beak, after Leo the Lion has crushed the serpents head!

The Raven here is used as a picture of final destruction of not only Satan, but all of his seed, which includes all who take the mark of the beast - the 666; in other words all who choose the

Babylon system of sin and death; rather than the Messiah's offer of redemption and life. To the former, the Ravens (along with other scavenger birds) will be summoned and used by God as His "mop up" crew. They will feed on the dead bodies of those killed during the coming Day of the Lord's Anger.

The following is the actual passage, and *sorry*, it isn't any less graphic than my rendition!

"Then I saw an angel standing in the sun; and he cried with a loud voice, saying to all the birds that fly in the midst of heaven, "Come and gather together for the supper of the great God, that you may eat the flesh of kings, the flesh of captains, the flesh of mighty men, the flesh of horses and of those who sit on them, and the flesh of all people, free and slave, both small and great." Revelation 19:17-18

Why Does Merciful God Orchestrate the Apocalypse?

The carnal spirit inside us all has blinded many from the things that make for peace - fellowship with God. Fallen man continues to embrace the spirit of Babylon which permeates the churches, nations, governments of the world, and the hearts of the carnal minded. Justice demands judgment.

When considering the wrath of God, keep in mind however that the wine of the wrath of God almighty is no more horrific than what the Antichrist will inflict upon all of those innocent souls that place their allegiance in God and refuse to align themselves with this fallen world which in the time of the end will be totally demon possessed. The lost souls (the billions that are possessed by the carnal mind) will blame and curse God for their calamities - repentance no longer crosses their minds which are now totally controlled by the serpent. Remember that God and all that he created are balanced by the laws of polarity. God will balance the scales of justice against Satan - that my friend is the reason for the apocalypse!

The apocalypse must occur to restore the perfect balance that Satan and sin corrupted.

When did the Cosmic Battle for Your Soul Begin?

The Garden of Eden is representative of the cosmic battle going on since the dawn of this age. In the midst of the Garden were the Tree of Life and also the tree of the Knowledge of Good and Evil! Jesus represents the Tree of Life and Satan the Tree of the Knowledge of Good and Evil. The cosmic battle in the heavens that the Zodiac signs confirm is for our soul and our allegiance. We have one choice - we can't choose both sides. This is the central theme of this age and why both trees were smack in the middle of the Garden. Man chose Satan when they ate of His tree and that is why man lost the immortality associated with the tree of life, and struggles with the carnal desires of the flesh which is mortal. Mankind chose death (in the literal and spiritual sense) when they chose the wrong side!

Because of original sin, Satan was lowered from the heavens to the earthly realm and is now one with man. But we can be liberated.

Recap of the Message behind the Zodiac Signs:

The first sign is of Virgo the Virgin carrying the seed of the Messiah who will bring forth God's redemptive plan for mankind, which carries forward into Libra, the Scales. Just like in the bible, we see in the Zodiac signs numerous attempts by the serpent to undermine God's redemptive plan for mankind. We see the ongoing battle between good and evil within various signs.

We see the conflict beginning with Scorpio the scorpion, which is the first rendition of the serpent (Satan). It bruises the heal of Orphiuchus (a picture of Jesus); but Jesus crushes the scorpions (Satan's) head.

The serpent is then pictured struggling to steal the crown off of Orphiuchus (the Messiah's) head. But Orphiuchus has a firm grip on the serpent assuring that it cannot get a hold of His crown.

Satan again shows up, this time as Cetus the Sea Monster, who is pictured trying to destroy (devour) Pisces the Fishes (the church of God - all Christians). **Revelation 12:9; 17.**

Again we see Satan defeated as the dead remains of the devourer that was destroyed by Orion (Jesus). Orion is pictured holding the dead carcass of a lion - which is Satan beast that devours.

Finally, we see him roaming around in the sign of Leo the Lion in the form of Hydra the giant serpent. Hydra covers ***one third*** of the star in the heavens just like Satan convinced ***one third*** of the angels in heaven to rebel against God! But in this final battle with the serpent, we see him destroyed threefold in the constellation of Leo the Lion:

1) Satan is crushed by the feet of Leo the Lion.
2) Satan is destroyed by the fire from the cup of the wrath of God.
3) Satan is devoured by the scavenger birds of the air as depicted by Corvus the Raven.
So the message written in the heavens is that Jesus will crush the head of Satan, and Christ will reign as King of Kings. That is why the true message behind Revelation is not one of doom and gloom, but rather, a message of celebration for those who believe that Christ is their Lord and savior. Those who side with Jesus are assured victory by the creator of the Universe,

and are guaranteed a crown of victory in heaven. These will reign as kings and priests with Christ forever:

"You have made them to be a kingdom and priests to serve our God, and they will reign on the earth."
Revelation 5:10

Chapter 15 - The Myth and the Truth Surrounding the Constellations

In this chapter I want to show the difference between the mythical message of the Zodiac signs and the divine message and scriptural message behind the signs. So I will share first the truth behind the Zodiac as interpreted by the word of God, and the Mythical message as interpreted by the carnal minded man. So let's get started.

1. **VIRGO, the Virgin**

The Truth
A young virgin bearing a child. She holds a branch in her right hand and an ear of corn in her left. The "seed" of the woman is to bring the Savior - Jesus Christ the Messiah.
Corresponding verses: Genesis 3:15; Rev. 12:1

The Myth:
Also known in mythology as Astraea. She represents justice and the scales of Libra are positioned next to Virgo in the heavens.

2. LIBRA, the Scales

The Truth:
This is a figure of a pair of balances, with one side up and the other down, as in the act of weighing. All creation is subject to sin and death - we are lacking, and blemished. But the redemption offered by the Lamb of God wipes away the sins of man - thus balancing our scales so that we can live as one in Christ.

The Myth:
Libra represents a balance of scales and justice. In Greek mythology Libra commemorated Mochis, the inventor of weights and measures. Libra also represented the balances of

Astraea, the goddess of Justice, in which the fate of all mortal men must eventually be weighed. The Egyptians identified Libra with the scales in which the human heart is weighed after death. In India, Libra was also known as a balance, shown in their Zodiac as a kneeling man holding up a pair of scales.

3. SCORPIO the Scorpion

The Truth
This figure of a giant insect, with its tail and sting uplifted in anger, as if striking. The sting of sin and death via the carnal mind that infects every man. It is attempting to sting a man in the heal (Orion) but instead it is crushed by this mighty man. Clearly the man is Jesus and this Crab is Satan who strikes Jesus heal as God prophesied in **Genesis 1:15.**

The Myth
In this rendition, the scorpion is believed to be responsible for the death of the great hunter Orion, because of his boast that he could defeat any beast.
Note: Hmmm, this is the exact opposite of the truth since Orion can indeed and will destroy all of the beasts in the Zodiac - since Messiah is the true representation of Orion.

4. SAGITTARIUS

The Truth:
The Archer: is the figure of a horse with the head of a man with a drawn bow and arrow pointed at the Scorpion. The man riding the horse (Centaur) is a picture of Jesus the mighty conqueror (the archer), who through the Holy Spirit can rip Satan's influences right out of our heart.

The Myth:
Is representative of the gentle centaur Chiron (half horse - half human), that was accidentally shot and wounded by Hercules.

Note: So what is the message here; what can mankind gain from this? Nothing!

5. CAPRICORN

The Truth

This is the figure of a goat at the point of death, which has a hinder part of a fish that is full of vigor as if it is about to be born out of the goat. This is a sign of redemption through the death and resurrection of Messiah. A sign of Jesus seed - the body of Christ; the church that would evolve out of the Lamb of God's *sacrificial death* for the redemption of sin.

The Myth

This depicts the result of the sudden appearance of the earthborn giant Typhoeus. As a sacrifice, Bacchus who was feasting on the Nile, jumped into the river. The part of him that was under water was changed into a fish, while his upper body was transformed into a goat. In gratitude over Bacchus sacrifice, *Zeus* then placed the shape of Bacchus in the heavens in gratitude.

NOTE: We see again that credit is being given to the false god **Zeus (Satan)** for creation of this heavenly body instead of the true God!

6. AQUARIUS

The Truth

Water is a symbol of the Holy Spirit since it cleanses the body of its sinful nature. Aquarius is a symbol of God's pouring out of the Holy Spirit upon His elect. So this symbol represents the body of Christ and the fullness of the Lord. This picture represents the Lord's promise to pour out His Holy Spirit for all who thirst and call out His name.

The Myth

While tending his father's flocks on Mount Ida, Ganymede was spotted by **Zeus**. The king of gods became enamored of the boy and flew down to the mountain in the form of a large bird, whisking Ganymede away to the heavens. Ever since, the boy has served as cupbearer to the gods.

NOTE: What a perversion of the true meaning of Aquarius. And **Zeus (Satan)** again is behind this and he is given credit for creating this sign! Satan always wanted to be God, to be a creator. Are we seeing a trend here?

7- PISCES, the Fishes:

The Truth

The two fishes are clearly a representation of the church. This connection between fish and the body of Christ is sprinkled throughout the gospels. The sea represents the lowest depths of civilization where sin and death abide. So casting the fish out of the sea is representative of being born again, and rescued out of the sea of depravity.

The Myth

The giant Typhoeus appears again, so all the gods scramble for cover. Even Zeus is scared and transforms into a ram. Hermes becomes an ibis; Apollo takes on the shape of a crow; Artemis a cat; and Bacchus hides as a goat . Aphrodite and her son Eros were bathing on the banks of the Euphrates River that day, and took on the shapes of a pair of fish to escape danger. Minerva later commemorates the event by placing the figures of two fish amongst the stars.

Note: With so many gods in charge, the message here is that there is no one God in control of anything!

8. ARIES, the Ram or Lamb:

A clear picture of the Lamb of God that takes away the sins of the world.
In the Old Testament, before the Messiah, atonement for sin required an animal sacrifice - such as a lamb or ram.   But Jesus would make the animal sacrifices obsolete, through His blood at the cross - the perfect sacrifice that covers the sins of the world.

The Myth

In Mythology this represents the ram that was sacrificed to present a golden fleece to king Aeetes.

9. Taurus the Bull

The Truth

There is no doubt that the sign of Taurus is one of judgment, and the going forward of Christ to enact judgment. This coming judgment is referred to as the "wrath of the Lamb" in the book of Revelation.

The Myth

Represents the bull form taken on by Zeus to seduce Europa, princess of Phenicia.
Note: Hmmm, perfect example of Satan who is "the great seducer"!

10. GEMINI the Twins

The Truth

The twins are a picture of the law of polarity which requires perfect balance in the universe and in the character of the creator. All creation operates in a state of balance, under God's control.

The Myth

Represents the twin brothers Castor and Pollux. Both were mothered by Leda, and as such were brothers of Helen. They had different fathers. In one night, Leda was made pregnant both by **_Zeus_** in the form of a swan and by her husband, the king Tyndarus of Sparta.

Note: Sounds to me like the perfect depiction of a dysfunctional family, with Zeus (the devil) of course being the head of that house!

11. CANCER the Crab

The Truth

Like the Crab, the church is born of water and of the Holy Spirit - which is symbolized as water. And as the crab can live in two environments (land and water), the church also resides in two environments; earth and heaven. Our body belongs on earth but our spirit belongs in heaven. Of course it is not a free trip; to make it to heaven our mind must be transformed. With the help of the Holy Spirit we can transform our mind from carnally minded to spiritually minded.

The Myth

In mythology it represents that crab that was sent to harass Hercules by nipping on his heels Hercules eventually crushed it with his feet. It is positioned between the constellations Leo and Gemini.

NOTE: Almost picture perfect - except that it is the Messiah that is pictured here and not a mythical hero and idol called Hercules.

12. LEO, the Lion

The Truth

The figure of a great Lion with its feet over the head of Hydra the Serpent, is a picture of the Lion of the tribe of Judah defeating the Satan the serpent once and for all. Satan is defeated and Christ is now the Victor; King of Kings and Lord of Lords.

The Myth

In mythology it is representative of the Nemean lion that was killed by Hercules, and that Hercules wore the skin of the Lion as protection!

Note: Another distortion of the truth, since Satan, masquerading as Hercules destroys the Lion, which of course is the opposite of the fact that in the end The Lion crushes the head of the serpent.
As you can clearly see, the mythological misrepresentations of the Zodiac offer absolutely nothing. No logical conclusion, no divine explanation, only mythical stories and distortions of the truth. It becomes quite evident from studying the Mythical accounts, that the fictitious characters are never divine representations but rather demonic representations - such as false gods, idols, and manmade heroes and characters. For example **Zeus is not God** as the mythical account implies, rather, Zeus is Satan - masquerading as the God who placed

these zodiac signs in the heavens! What is a picture of Jesus and God, Satan has corrupted to a false picture of him!

Other Myths, False Signs, and Supernatural Spirits

The following are excerpts from my book: **"*Aliens, Fallen Angels, Nephilim and the Supernatural*"**. I want to share some of this information with you because it is so important that we recognize all of the fiery darts that the prince of darkness shoots at us from all angles to confuse and torment our minds. These Satanic influences are not just limited to sin, lust or temptation.

Satan attacks from all angles including the media (including music, internet porn, etc.), family issues, addictions, disease, panic attacks, emotions like fear, governments, leaders, universities, false religions, myths (as we have just covered), false prophets, and false signs from above and here on earth, among others.

Satan will always attack us from where we are most vulnerable. As we grow in spirit it will be much easier for us to discern when he is attacking us (whether mentally, or physically). He is out for blood; he wants that blood of Jesus (and the Holy Spirit)out of our minds body and soul.

So let's begin....

The Nephilim
We know from the book of Genesis that in the beginning God intended for every life form to re-produce in its own kind (**Genesis 1 verses 11, 12, 24-25**). And in **Genesis 1:26** God reveals that he made us in his own image.

God then reveals in **Genesis chapter 6:1-4** how Satan immediately attacked the DNA of God's creation, which God made in his own image, by having fallen angels mate with women creating unholy mutants (called the Nephilim) attempting to corrupt the DNA of man!

Genesis 6:4 (This is all Pre-Flood) reveals the following: "there were giants in the earth in those days; and also after that." Giants being the Nephilim. Here is the whole verse: ***"There were giants on the earth in those days, and also afterward, when the sons of God came in to the daughters of men and they bore children to them. Those were the mighty men who were of old, men of renown."*** Genesis 6:4

Before the great flood, a secret hybrid race of fallen angels breeding with human women was conspired by Satan to circumvent God's plans for man.

Under Satan, a race of Nephilim giants was spawned. Satan wanted these giants to subdue mankind and take over the world (sort of like what Satan possessed Hitler, wanted the Germanic people under Nazi control to morph into). And this breeding of this race of god-men or supermen is an essential Satan inspired theme of all occult-based religions throughout history. Adolph Hitler hoped to use this "Science of Eugenics" to scientifically breed a new master race of supermen or god-men.

Because of this unholy union, God had to destroy the whole earth with a great flood in order to destroy the Nephilim seed and fallen man who had willingly corrupted the DNA of almost all mankind, save Noah and his immediate family. So if Aliens exist, perhaps they are the offspring of the Nephilim. It is important here to note that these creatures were descendents of the fallen angels, and so upon their death, their spirits would remain alive on earth and would take on the role of demons.

As already noted, ***the Nephilim are the result of fallen angels*** mating with women and thus polluting the gene pool. Prior to this abomination, man's DNA was perfect. That is why we read in the ancient scriptures how Adam and some of his offspring lived upwards of 900 years. There apparently was no or little disease before the great flood (Genesis 5:5). Then after the flood man's lifespan was reduced to around 70 years or so.

Researchers in the field believe that these Nephilim originally grew to over 36 feet tall and gradually in time would grow smaller to around 10 feet or so. This adds credence to the story of Goliath during David's time (1 Samuel 17:49).

After the great flood apparently, some Nephilim DNA did manage to survive because there remained some giants in the land during Moses and Abraham's time. The giant Goliath and the Giborim are examples of Nehilim offspring. Also, the nations that occupied the land of Israel (the Hittites, Jebusites, Amorites, Hivites, etc.) that God commanded the Israelites to fully destroy their entire families - including men, wives and children, most likely had to be totally destroyed because they were descendants of the Nephilim, and had the corrupted DNA of the Nephilim!

Aliens

Satan wants us to think that Aliens exist, and that they are more intelligent than us, and that we are not a special creation with a divine spirit - unlike anything else. He refuses to accept that **_WE, and NOT Satan,_** are created in God's image.

And to add insult to injury, these "Aliens" are depicted as these ugly little grayish greenish monsters that are smarter and more special than us...hmmm! Don't you already discern something wrong and outright silly with this part of the "Alien conspiracy"?

Nephilim like mutations were also produced through the mixing of human DNA with animals. As if the Nephilim were not enough, Satan had the fallen angels teach men how to

experiment with and mix the DNA of humans with animals so as to create creatures that were part human and part animal - just like modern science is doing behind the scene today!
This explains why in ancient hieroglyphics and writings we see images depicting many beings that were part human and part animal.

So if Aliens do exist, then they must be demonic creatures, perhaps offspring of the Nephilim race, mixing of DNA, or a byproduct thereof.

But we know better, right? **WE** are created in the image of our creator, and so it is a satanic delusion to think that if we are an image of God, that aliens or any other demonic mutation of what God made perfect, can be superior in any manner over God's children!!!

UFO's and Alien Abductions

UFO sightings seem to be more present during major events such as Israel's formation in 1948, and when Israel re-captured Jerusalem in1967, (are these UFO's actually Satan's version of spy satellites being operated by demons?). Obviously Satan is interested in anything related to Israel, which is God's prophetic time piece. So are we alone in the Universe? Nope - but the "extraterrestrials" may not be what you think - they more than likely are the devil's minions (demons, fallen angels, etc.) that occupy the 2nd heaven (the skies), and who masquerade in all sorts of forms..

I believe that if Aliens do indeed exist, and do indeed abduct humans, then these creatures are controlled by Satan and their purpose is to alter human DNA (just like in ancient times). We do not just hear "rumors" of human abductions, we also hear and read reports about cattle that seem to have been left dead in many fields void of blood and their internal organs. Whether by Devil worshippers, Chupacabra, or aliens, they all have the same footprint - Satan doing his dirty work, trying to corrupt God's perfect creations.

The blood is the life force essential for the flesh, to sustain physical life in the first heaven (earth). So these demonic spirits may not be able to manifest into a physical mutation, without this human or animal blood. This would explain human and animal abductions, if indeed UFO abductions are taking place!

The Mayans of the past, and all devil worshippers require human blood sacrifices to appease their gods, and all ancient cultures like these were demonic and occult in nature. This would explain human and animal abductions, if indeed UFO abductions are taking place!

Demons

We know from the bible that these spirits do exist. They are fallen angels.
they may also be the disembodied spirits of the Nephilim which, which in order to live on, have to occupy a human body or a biological suit (like grey suits; ET and other mutations). It's all about the joining of 2 species; in this case a demonic mutation.

Fallen Angels
Aliens, if they do exist, may actually be a misidentification of fallen angels.
Remember that there are no entities or intelligent creatures except those spoken of clearly in the Bible. Anything not identified for us in God's word should be considered a fabrication of man influenced by the carnal mind (Satan).

Keep in mind that angels can take the form of a man (and other creature like forms for that matter). Because of his supernatural powers, it is easy for the devil to trick many (unfamiliar with the word of God) into believing in Aliens, extraterrestrial life, Zombies, vampires, the boogey man and just about anything our incredibly creative minds want to believe!

Mythological Characters, gods, and the Heroes of Renown

All these Greek "god(s)"; stories of renown may be the intentional or unintentional worship of the Nephilim (Idol, demon, and Satan Worship). This is just as Satan would have wanted to happen, and this practice of idol worship sadly goes on today!

In the last days, knowledge will Increase

Knowledge is great, especially if used for good purposes and to develop our spirit mind and not for evil purposes. There are a lot of very smart people through the ages who have used their knowledge to inflict pain, suffering, and many other evil acts.

Technological advances can be used for good, and in some cases they are. They create so many opportunities to expand our knowledge base and to communicate. But here we are, in these last days and our world is totally distracted by all the pleasures of the many technological gadgets and toys of these modern times.

Today's laptops store more information than the Cray computers of the 1950's! This technological explosion is great as long as the world uses it for good, and let's hope we use it better than with the development of Nuclear fusion - the later being an explosion that none of us want to experience!

Daniel prophesied that "knowledge" would increase exponentially in the last days.

"Many shall run to and fro and Knowledge shall increase"
Daniel 12:4

So since Satan represented the Tree of the Knowledge of Good and Evil, it stands to reason that this advanced knowledge will be used in the last days for evil purposes! I offer the following examples of how...

knowledge can and will be used for all kinds of abominations:

- From 1900 we went from horse and buggy to planes, and rocket propelled probes past Pluto, the Hubel telescope, Nuclear Bombs, unimagined computing power, and many more technological advances. More than 2053 nuclear bombs have gone off from 1945 to 1998!
- Science is rushing to achieve what is termed as the "Singularity"; this is where machines become smarter and more intellectual than humans. This is also termed as Artificial Intelligence, or artillects. This of course is another satanic plot to replace man with part human part machine mutations, and of course to try to reduce humans as mutations void of God's spirit, like the walking dead (zombies), and to delude mankind into thinking that we are an inferior race and that Satan has the power to improve on God's creation. You cannot make something that is perfect, more perfect.

- Mankind wants to become immortal without God. A recent Time magazine article said that **by 2045 man becomes immortal as we become "manchines";** part man yet part machine.

- Trans humanism is the idea that we can permanently alter the human race with artificial intelligence systems so that we can be supernatural; to create a superior model of humans with robotics, etc. like what Hitler wanted.

- Social media can be fun and a great way to stay in touch. But rather than using these modern day tools to share the good news of the Kingdom of God to this fallen world, most would rather share pictures, jokes and anything, as long as it has nothing to do with the God of the bible. Everybody is so distracted with these high tech toys that many fail to recognize or choose to ignore the signs of the times that Jesus Christ outlined in the signs of the times foretold in **Mathew chapter 24**.

If you found this topic interesting and would like to research this area further, you should pick up a copy of my book: **"*Aliens, Fallen Angels, Nephilim and the Supernatural*"
Now in chapter 16, we are going to cover significant divine signs which are scheduled to start (according to NASA studies in April 2014 - just before this book comes out! So be ready for some exciting stuff in the next chapter!**

Chapter 16 - The Blood Moon Signs and the Apocalypse

From the very beginning God revealed that he created the stars in the heavens not only for the telling of the seasons but also for signs (**Genesis 1:14**). There are six Great Signs in the heavens that will begin in 2014 that perhaps warn that the Great Tribulation may be imminent!

The Four Blood Moons - Tetrad

NASA scientists have confirmed that in 2014 and 2015 there will be a series of blood moons - four in all, and there will also be a solar eclipse in the middle of the blood moons. A total solar eclipse is referred to as a blood moon because the event casts a red shadow on the moon. When several (four) blood moons occur within a short period (a two year span) it is called a Tetrad.

There have only been about three of these in recent history. These occur when God wants to alert the world of a significant event a-coming. Now when these Tetrads occur around Jewish feast days, they usually precede very significant world changing events.

The History of the Blood Moons

1492 - Tetrads occurred during Jewish feast days in 1492. In addition to the discovery of America, during this period, the Spanish inquisition led to the torture, martyrdom and expulsion of Jewish citizens who did not convert to Catholicism.

1949 - Four blood moons (Tetrad) next appeared just before the nation of Israel was rebirth in 1948. No other nation in history has reemerged once totally destroyed.

1967-1968 This Tetrad occurred during the year that Israel recaptured Jerusalem after almost nineteen hundred years.

2014 and 2015 - It will now happen again starting in 2014 and ending in 2015! And again, it will occur during Jewish feast days - clearly a sign from God - that we better pay attention because it means that something BIG is about to happen.

<u>**Below is when these heavenly signs are expected to take place**</u>:

- **April 15th 2014** - **Blood Moon** (on the Passover feast day)
- **October 8th 2014** - **Blood Moon** (on the Feast of Tabernacles)
- **March 20th 2015** - **Solar Eclipse** (Month 1 in the Hebrew calendar)
- **April 2nd 2015** - **Blood Moon** (on the Passover feast day)
- **September 13th 2015** - **partial Eclipse** (on the Feast of Trumpets)
- **September 27th 2015** - **Blood Moon** (on the feast of Tabernacles)

A complete solar eclipse in the midst of 4 total lunar eclipses (blood moons) is a signal of a significant event that will impact the whole world.

The fact that the blood moons (total lunar eclipses) are to take place is not as significant as the fact that they are expected to occur during Jewish feast days. As a result, they may indeed be a great sign from God the Almighty signaling the beginning of the apocalypse (also referred to as the great tribulation, day of the Lord, the time of Jacob's troubles, and Armageddon), or some other very ominous event(s) leading to the tribulation period.

Blood moons that occur during Jewish feast days are usually a bad omen for Israel, whereby a solar eclipse in the midst of these blood moons, may be a bad omen for the whole world. We are getting a combination of six of these in the span of two years, starting this year - 2014!

Perhaps these **blood moons** scheduled to commence on April 15, 2014 and scheduled to conclude on September 27 2015, will fulfill the following Old Testament prophecies...

"The sun will be turned to darkness and the moon to blood before the coming of the great and dreadful day of the Lord." (Joel 2:31)
"The sun shall be turned into darkness, and the moon into blood, before the coming of the great and awesome day of the Lord." (Acts 2:20)

The Shemittah Year:

A **Shemittah year** occurs every seven years, and it was established by God for Israel to allow the land to rest so that it could produce at maximum potential during the following six year cycle (just like a Sabbath does for mankind). **It is a time where God blesses or judges nations based on their observance of this and His other laws.**

Below is what has happened recently to America during the 7th year Shemittah cycles:

- **9/11/2001** was a Shemittah year
- **2008** was another of these years, and saw the potential collapse of America's financial markets.
 - **2015** The next Shemittah year is scheduled for **2015**
The fact that a Shemittah year will also occur in 2015, beginning in September 2014 (The feast of Trumpets - the Jewish New Year called Rosh Hashanah) is extremely significant. The Feast of Trumpets is celebrated on the first day of the seventh month (Leviticus 23:24-25). It is a day of remembrance and the sounding of the shofar (trumpet). The blowing of the shofar is a call to repentance.

Obviously, with these signs occurring in rapid succession and during significant dates, it is clear that something big is about to happen. Could these signs all portend of the beginning of sorrows; the tribulation period also called the Apocalypse?

The Lord's Feast Days and their significance:

God established certain days to be set aside and celebrated in commemoration of God's relationship with all mankind - through His chosen people and nation; that were intended to be an example to all peoples and nations. These feast days, in and of themselves, reveal God's master plan for not just Israel and the Jews, but for all mankind as well.

In Genesis we can clearly see that God defines each day beginning in the evening and ending the following evening (evening to evening). Read Genesis 1:3; 1:6; 1:13; 1:19; 1:23; 1:31. The **Hebrew calendar (God's calendar)** starts all days on the evening before that day - *and Aligns more perfectly to God's timeline, than the other "man-made" Calendars.*

Of the feast days two are very significant when dealing with the coming blood moons; Passover (Pesach) and (the Feast of Tabernacles - Sukkot).

Passover:

Passover starts on the 15th day of Nissan. It is the first month of the Hebrew year. Leviticus 23:4-5; Exodus 12:14. It is a lamb sacrifice commemorating the Exodus of the children of Israel from Egyptian bondage (Exodus 1-15). The blood of the lamb spared their life, as the angel of death passed over the home of those who applied the blood of the lamb on their door. Clearly this is symbolic of Messiah Jesus, whom the Jews rejected, who is the Lamb of God who takes away the sins of the world (John 1:29; 1 Peter 1:19; Revelation 5:6-13).

The Feast of Tabernacles (Sukkot):

This feast begins on the 15th day of the Hebrew month of Tishri. It is also referred to as the feast of booths (tents). This festival commemorates the 40 years that the children of Israel wandered in the desert living in tents(Leviticus 23:34-43). It is a time of thanksgiving and rest to celebrate God's provision and protection. It is symbolic with the time of peace whereby the Messiah reigns with His people - **the coming Millennium** (Hebrews 4:8-9; Isaiah 11:10). *Could this be what the coming Blood Moons be alerting us to*?

Each of The Blood Moons of 2014 and 2015 will occur during one of the above feast days. So Blood moons will occur during Passover 2014 and 2015, and during the feast of Tabernacles of 2014 and 2015!

Prophecies about the Coming Tribulation Period / Apocalypse

Note: For much more on the coming Tribulation/Apocalypse please consider reading my new book: *"Revelation Mysteries Decoded - Unlocking the Secrets of the Coming Apocalypse"*

Not only do the **Zodiac signs** confirm that just before the time of the end there will be one more great confrontation between the forces of good and evil that will shake the very foundations of the world, and many (**Billions**) will perish. The aforementioned coming signs in **2014 and 2015** may perhaps signal the beginning of the apocalypse (referred to as the great Tribulation period - a 7 year period before the end of this age), is just around the corner!

Mathew 24 is one of the most important chapters of the Bible relative to end of days prophecies; and these prophesies are coming from none other than Messiah Jesus. **Who better** than the returning Messiah to turn to for clues regarding the time of the end scenario!
Below I will cover the entire chapter with some key points:

"Now as He sat on the Mount of Olives, the disciples came to Him privately, saying, "Tell us, when these things will be? And what will be the sign of Your coming, and of the end of the age?"
"And Jesus answered and said to them: "Take heed that no one deceives you. For many will come in My name, saying, 'I am the Christ,' and will deceive many. And you will hear of wars and rumors of wars. See that you are not troubled; for all these things must come to pass, but the end is not yet. For nation will rise against nation, and kingdom against kingdom. And there will be famines, pestilences, and earthquakes in various places. All these are the beginning of sorrows." (Mathew 24:2-7)

Notes:
In **Mathew 24:7** Jesus may not just be referring to global skirmishes but also a massive cosmic battle between the principalities in the supernatural realm. This is revealed in **Revelation 12:7**: *"And war broke out in heaven: Michael and his angels fought with the dragon; and the dragon and his angels fought, but they did not prevail, nor was a place found for them in heaven any longer."*
We must realize after all, this will be the final battle before Messiah returns victoriously so Satan will go all out against God and mankind. He will use every dirty trick in his book to take out as much of mankind as possible.

And just like Hitler blamed his own people and the German citizens for losing the war, Satan will turn against even those who take his mark. Only the foolish that lack wisdom and knowledge will believe and find a sense of security in taking the mark of the beast (666), and making a perpetual covenant with Satan.

Modern science has made great strides to rid the world of many of the *pestilences* that plagued mankind over the last 6,000 years. However, these advances will be countered by super bugs that and plagues in the coming apocalypse. Today, scientists are already warning us of mutated viruses that we currently have no vaccines to counter them with. It is a time-bomb waiting to detonate. Assuredly there will be pestilences in the near future as Jesus warned in **Mathew 24:7**

The 3rd rider of the apocalypse (**Revelation Ch. 6**) riding the black horse, carries a pair of scales. This may be symbolic of a period of financial ruin, inflation, and famine. Perhaps due to the plagues that will afflict the earth during the apocalypse, there will be a massive shortage of food so that a day's wages will only buy a quart of wheat - I guess that would be about a small loaf of bread to feed a family for just a day.

The United States of America, the once "breadbasket of the world" is no longer a nation that can offer food security to the world. In 1935 this nation boasted 6.8 million farms, whereas today less than 2 million remain (U.S. Dept. of Agriculture statistics). The small farmer is being driven out by the large conglomerates and our foreign "economic partners" who are also **buying large chunks of America's farmland**.

"Then they will deliver you up to tribulation and kill you, and you will be hated by all nations for My name's sake. And then many will be offended, will betray one another, and will hate one another. Then many false prophets will rise up and deceive many. And because lawlessness will abound, the love of many will grow

cold. But he who endures to the end shall be saved. And this gospel of the kingdom will be preached in the entire world as a witness to all the nations, and then the end will come."

Note: During the tribulation period, the inhabitants of the earth will have become so deluded and possessed by Satan, that they will hate all Christians and Jews (and each other for that matter). They will also hate and curse God, and blame God for all of the judgments that are loosed upon the earth (**Rev. 16:9**)

"Therefore when you see the 'abomination of desolation,' spoken of by Daniel the prophet, standing in the holy place" (whoever reads, let him understand), "then let those who are in Judea flee to the mountains. Let him who is on the housetop not go down to take anything out of his house. And let him who is in the field not go back to get his clothes. But woe to those who are pregnant and to those who are nursing babies in those days! And pray that your flight may not be in winter or on the Sabbath. For then there will be great tribulation, such as has not been since the beginning of the world until this time, no, nor ever shall be. <u>And unless those days were shortened, no flesh would be saved; but for the elect's sake those days will be shortened.</u>"

Note: It will get so bad that God will need to intervene and end the bloodbath before all life is destroyed.

"Then if anyone says to you, 'Look, here is the Christ!' or 'There!' do not believe it. For false christs and false prophets will rise and show great signs and wonders to deceive, if possible, even the elect. See, I have told you beforehand."
"Therefore if they say to you, 'Look, He is in the desert!' do not go out; or 'Look, He is in the inner rooms!' do not believe it. For as the lightning comes from the east and flashes to the west, so also will the coming of the Son of Man be. For wherever the carcass is, there the eagles will be gathered together." Mathew 24:23-28

NOTE(s): Jesus is emphasizing here that we must not believe who the media, religious system, and the world is worshipping as the messiah, because the Antichrist may even be proclaiming that the false prophet is Jesus the Messiah (hence the *"Blasphemy"* that he is accused of engaging - in Revelation) who is now walking on earth and that the one world religion will be blessed by this false Messiah. Since the world is void of the Holy Spirit and the world, they will worship the false prophet.

Prior to the Lord's return, a fallen world will seek and worship just about any false prophet that claims solutions or provides answers (or lies) or solutions (deception). Since they are starved of the knowledge of the word, they will fall for anything - including all of the Antichrist's lies and deception. **Mathew 24:26-29**
As a result there will be famines, earthquakes and epidemics throughout the world.

"Immediately after the tribulation of those days the sun will be darkened, and the moon will not give its light; the stars will fall from heaven, and the powers of the heavens will be shaken. Then the sign of the Son of Man will appear in heaven, and then all the tribes of the earth will mourn, and they will see the Son of Man coming on the

*clouds of heaven with power and great glory. And He will
send His angels with a great sound of a trumpet, and they
will gather together His elect from the four winds, from
one end of heaven to the other."*

Note: Jesus reveals that all those walking on earth claiming
to be the Messiah are part of Satan's end day deceptions, and
that the TRUE Messiah will appear descending from the
heavens and will not be walking on the earth until the earth is
cleansed with the fire (with the Cup of the Wrath of God).

*"Now learn this parable from the fig tree: When its branch
has already become tender and puts forth leaves, you
know that summer is near. So you also, when you see all
these things, know that it is near—at the
doors! Assuredly, I say to you, this generation will by no
means pass away till all these things take place. Heaven
and earth will pass away, but My words will by no means
pass away."*

Note: Most scholars agree that this prophecy of the fig tree is
representative of Israel which was reborn as a State in 1948.
If a generation is 70 years, than this takes us to around 2018
as perhaps the beginning of the tribulation/apocalypse!

*"But of that day and hour no one knows, not even the
angels of heaven, but My Father only. But as the days of
Noah were, so also will the coming of the Son of Man
be. For as in the days before the flood, they were eating*

and drinking, marrying and giving in marriage, until the day that Noah entered the ark, and did not know until the flood came and took them all away, so also will the coming of the Son of Man be. Then two men will be in the field: one will be taken and the other left. Two women will be grinding at the mill: one will be taken and the other left. Watch therefore, for you do not know what hour your Lord is coming. But know this that if the master of the house had known what hour the thief would come, he would have watched and not allowed his house to be broken into. Therefore you also be ready, for the Son of Man is coming at an hour you do not expect."

Note: Indeed, nobody knows the day and the hour, but we can most certainly discern the signs of the time. Otherwise the Lord and the prophets would not have gone to such great lengths to describe what the end time signs would be.

Coming Judgments and Calamities During the Tribulation Period:

The Deadly Four

No nation or group of nations can prepare or defend against the certain destruction that can come about from any of the following four calamities:

1) A **Nuclear exchange** most certainly create the calamities prophesied to occur during the tribulation period. These weapons of mass destruction have changed the game and are weapons that can fulfill most of the plagues and judgments mentioned in the apocalypse.

2) Even without these weapons of mass destruction all it takes is one or more mile wide **meteor or asteroid impacts** to destroy our infrastructure, economies, and food sources.
3) Of course, the strong hand of God has no limitations - so God Himself could **rain down fire, hail and brimstone from heaven**. This is exactly what he did to Sodom and Gomorrah.
4) A worldwide earthquake.

God has used earthquakes in the past to get our attention. The US geological service recently reported that from **2008 to 2010 the earth has experienced 107,135** earthquakes. **America alone experienced 25,449** of these earthquakes, or slightly less than a quarter. Hmmm is God sending a message to **"the greatest nation on earth"**. Are we paying attention yet? The book of Revelation prophesizes that the last of the 7 great plagues will be a massive worldwide earthquake that may even topple mountains. **(Rev. 16:17-20)**

"You will be punished by the Lord of hosts
With thunder and <u>earthquake</u> and great noise,
With storm and tempest
And the <u>flame of devouring fire</u>." Isaiah 29:6

Why is God Warning us all of Impending Judgment?

I assume you already know the answer to this or at least have a good idea. But to make sure we are all clear on this, let me list some of the more significant reasons.

In a prior chapter I briefly explained that the earth needs to be cleansed before Messiah can return. In this section let's review some of the reasons why cleansing is required. Obviously **sin and immorality are a given**, so I will focus more on some of the main geo-political and societal reasons for the impending judgment upon the world.

1) Mankind's Rejection of the Lord: Just before the Lord's return **the inhabitants of the earth will have become such devil worshippers** that they even initiate a global feast day when God's two witnesses sent to the earth to evangelize the world are killed in the streets of Jerusalem by the Antichrist (Revelation 11:10). During the time of the end, the false prophet of the Antichrist will be performing great miracles, and because of the lack of knowledge of the truth, many will believe he is the long awaited Messiah.

These lost souls have rejected God and the word, and prefer the kingdom of Satan on earth, because they "think" they can do and get away with whatever they please, and whatever pleases them! *I know this sounds like science fiction; sadly it is NOT!*

2) Rampant Lawlessness. The Antichrist is referred to as "*the Lawless one*", so obviously there will be rampant lawlessness when he takes over during the tribulation period. But please do not think for a moment that lawlessness is relegated exclusively to the Tribulation period. It already runs rampant in the U.S. and throughout most of the world. Any doubts just watch the evening news. If it does not make you sick, sad, disgusted or depressed then you are already immune to this type of news - and that is not necessarily a good thing!
   The hardening of the spirit or the heart is the work of Satan and the media and government play a huge part in this evil transition of our collective minds.
So instead of immersing yourself into the filth that the media spews out, how about setting aside the world and immersing your mind and spirit in the word. I guarantee that this will make you feel much better.
   America, along with other nations, in their self righteous arrogance has made legal what God has forbidden from the beginning. And then mankind has the audacity to ask: *"Why would a loving God exact such great judgment upon our*

earth during the Apocalypse"?

God most assuredly will judge, and we as a society deserve it! Notwithstanding, God clearly explains the "why" to us in many places throughout the bible including in

<u>Isaiah 24:5-6:</u>

"The earth is polluted because of its inhabitants; who have transgressed the laws, violated the statutes and broke the everlasting covenant. Therefore a curse devours the earth; and its inhabitants are held guilty, therefore the inhabitants of the earth are burned, and few men are left."

<u>2) Dividing up God's land</u>: From the very beginning, the nations of this fallen earth have been "Hell-bent" (pun intended) on *dividing up God's land* (Jerusalem & Israel) that God gave to a chosen people. It is because Satan knows that the New heavens and new earth will be established in the area of Jerusalem, so he wants to take over that area so as to spoil God's plan.

<u>Throughout the bible, we see how God exacts Judgment upon those who try to divide Israel up</u>. We read of this in Joel 3:2, Nahum 1:2, Joshua 10:11 (God stoned to death the nations that tried to harm Israel during their 40 year journey in the wilderness), Haman (a Persian leader) and his family were hung to death when he tried to do the same to the sons of Israel. **Yet mankind still does not get it?**

<u>The word of God makes it clear that Jerusalem is the city of God</u>, and that the land of Israel was promised to the Jews. Let's read some of many verses whereby God tries to make this absolutely clear!

Psalm 132:13; psalm 48:1-2,8; Psalm 137:5-6; Psalm 121:4; Zechariah 14:1-2; Isaiah 24:23; John 10: 10. Genesis 17:18-19; Isaiah 54:1; Genesis 21:10; Galatians 4:21-31; Genesis 12:1-7; Genesis 13:14-15; Genesis 15:7-

10; 15:17-21; 22:16-17; Gen. 25:5-6; Gen. 26:1-6; Genesis 28:10-13; Exodus 3:8; Exodus 6:2-4; 6-8; Lev. 26:42; Numbers 34:2; Deuteronomy 1:8; Joshua 1:2-4; 1 Kings 8:36; 1 Chronicles 16:13-18; 2 Chronicles 6:25; Nehemiah 9:15; Psalm 105:8-11; Psalm 121:4; Isaiah 60:21

God declared thousands of years back that Israel would re-emerge as a nation. This was fulfilled in 1948. **Here are just a few prophetic references to this truth**: Jeremiah 30:3; Ezekiel 36:9-10; 24; 28; Amos 9:14-15; Zechariah 2:8

3) Persecution of Jews: From the first day that they became a unique race to God, the Jews have been a persecuted race.

Examples of this are:
- Pharaoh of Egypt
- King Nebuchadnezzar of Babylon (Iraq)
- Haman's plot (Persia/Iran)
- Epiphanies
- Titus
- Hadrian
- King Herod
- The Spanish Inquisition
- The Nazi Holocaust
- The Pogroms of Russia
- The 1967 and 1973 wars
- And I have probably missed some more.

The Nazi extermination camps where over six million innocent Jews and their families were sacrificed to the God of this world - Satan, is a testament of the everlasting hatred between the seed of Satan (all who worship and or do Satan's dirty work) and God's chosen people. The Nazi's called these atrocities **"the Final Solution" to the Jewish problem**.

There is a **GREAT** day of reckoning a-coming called the "**the Great Day of God The Almighty" and "the Day of the**

Lord's Anger"; which will be "GOD's FINAL SOLUTION" to mankind's problem!

In that day God will show the world and its inhabitants what He thinks of what mankind and their chosen leaders have done to His people and to His land - **God has NOT forgotten.** If you would like to have a better understanding of the apocalypse (the Great Tribulation) that appears to be just around the corner, you may want to consider getting a copy of my new book: *"Revelation Mysteries Decoded: Unlocking the Secrets of the Coming Apocalypse"*

Other Signs and Key Concepts:

Before we go to the final chapter, let's review some key concepts and some other interesting related data points:

- In Genesis 37:9-10 - Joseph (a symbol of Jesus) had a dream where the sun, moon and stars bowed before him. This meant that the 11 sons of Jacob and Jacob himself would bow down to him in Egypt as the 2nd in command. The Jews will bow before their Messiah when he returns for the second time; this time as the King of Kings.

- The Constellation Leo (symbolic of Jesus) contains the star **Regulus**. It is the brightest star in the constellation and one of the brightest stars in the night sky. It is appropriately referred to as the *"King star"*.

- Genesis 1:14 God created the heavens for a divine purpose. He positioned them for the telling of seasons and time - including prophetic signs.

- In the Jewish calendar time is circular (Ecclesiastes 1:9). The astronomical calendar (constellations) begins with Virgo (Virgin bearing a child - symbolic of the Messiah's birth **Luke 1:27),** and ends with Leo the Lion (Jesus the Lion of the Tribe of Judah **Rev. 5:5)**.

- **Satan perverted the signs** of heaven and corrupted their meaning, so that fallen man developed astrology and other occult practices so as to confuse mankind.

So mankind created many false gods based on the sun, moon, stars and the galaxies and has worshipped them over the ages so as to provoke God to anger, and thus secure the fate of mankind.

This is why God prohibited the worship of any images in the heavens, earth or underneath. **Romans 1:25**

- The ancient Greeks corrupted the meaning of God's signs in heaven. They perverted the truth *by idolizing the Nephilim* (the fallen angels) and worshipping them as gods such as Hercules, Zeus and Apollo, among many other gods.

- Satan influences the minds of world leaders and governments (**Ephesians 6:11-18**). This is why most nations, if not all, will fall prey to his delusion during the time of the end.

- Since the bible did not exist at the time, the heavenly signs served as God's word picture for early man, and serves as confirmation of His deity for modern times.

- **Josephus in the antiquities of the Jews** wrote that Seth, and some other descendants of Adam, had acquired special wisdom about the heavenly bodies, and that Adam had predicted long ago **that the world would be destroyed twice, once by water and eventually by fire.**

- **God revealed the heavenly secrets through Adam** and this knowledge was passed down to his descendants? This may explain why the ancients were so advanced in the study of astronomy and geometrics. This is also perhaps why the magi recognized the star of Bethlehem in the east and went to worship Jesus - **Mathew 2:2; 2:9**

- **The fallen angels and their Nephilim seed** (Genesis 6:1-3), taught astrology, worship of stars, and mythology. They corrupted God's word pictures in the heavens. They made Gods of the constellations, sun, moon and stars. From this evil seed grew the mythology that the Egyptians, Greeks, Romans, Babylonians and most other empires throughout this age embraced as part of their culture. These became the gods that they would worship.

- **Upon the destruction of the Jewish Temple in 70 AD**, a series of signs took place. Around that time a great comet swept the heavens for about one year over Israel. It is believed to have been **Haley's comet**. It appeared like a star resembling a sword in the heavens.

- **In Luke 21:25** Jesus prophesied the following before His return: *"There will be signs in the sun, moon and stars. On the earth, nations will be in anguish and perplexity at the roaring and tossing of the sea." This may refer to the coming Blood Moons.*

- **Haley's Comet** tends to appear four years before a major war that affects Israel. We already mentioned that **Haley's Comet appeared in AD 66**, four years before the destruction of the Jewish Temple. **It appeared in 1910, four years before WWI**. **It appeared again in 1988, four years before the gulf war**.

- **In 1917 near the end of World War I**, General Allenby librated Jerusalem from 400 years of Turkish rule, and also the Belfour declaration was issued giving Jews access to Palestine.

- In 1973 there were 7 eclipses (Sun and Moon together). The Yom Kippur war occurred that year. The Arab oil Embargo started that year, 28 nations suffered one of worst doubts in history, and scientists observed one of the largest solar explosion in the Sun.

- In 1996 there was a full Lunar eclipse (blood moon) over Jerusalem close to Passover on 4/3/96, and again on 9/26/96 during the Feast of Tabernacles. A total of three occurred in that year. This was the year that Israel was "persuaded" to surrender 97% of West Bank to their adversaries.

The Constellation Cetus in Greek mythology refers to a sea monster. The tail of this constellation covers 1/3rd of the stars of heaven (called the Southern Cross). Revelation 12:4 reveals how Lucifer, now Satan, caused one third of angels (**referred to as stars in Rev. 12:4**) to be cast out of heaven! Mere coincidence? Not!

The Antichrist was referred to in the signs: Cetus in Greek mythology, is a one half land and sea **monster**. It has a horn between the eyes and a star behind its neck. Cetus is referred to as the rebel, and also as the destroyer (just like Satan is referred to). **Revelation 13:1** reveals that another type of **monster** - the Antichrist (referred here as a beast) comes out of the sea and **Rev. 13:11** reveals that the false prophet comes out of the Earth. *The Antichrist also has a little horn (Daniel 7:8), just like Cetus*!

Revelation 1:20 refers to the mystery of 7 stars and lamp stands. This is referring to the seven churches. This also has a related cosmic sign. Church is a Greek feminine word meaning "Eklesia". There are 7 stars in the heavens which form a part of Pleiades M45; a 7 star formation on the neck of Taurus the bull. Speaking of Taurus, Jesus is holding the 7 stars in his right hand in Revelation representing the 7 churches. These 7 churches in revelation were located in

Turkey at the base of the "**TAURUS**" Mountains in Asia Minor
- *what a coincidence*!

In **Rev 12:1-3** we read of a great wonder in heaven; a woman
(symbolic of Israel) and a red dragon (Satan). Satan has
been at war with the nation of Israel from the moment it was
founded. Did you know that this supernatural battle has been
grafted in the heavens? When we study the constellations,
we see Draco the dragon (symbolic of Satan) with his eyes
fixated upon *Virgo* (symbolic of the Virgin with the Messiah
child), *as if it poised to attack and devour her*!

- **In Revelation 4:7** we see four living creatures worshipping
God. These are also pictured in the constellations.

The man (Aquarius) - represents Christ pouring out his holy
spirit
The Ox (Taurus the Bull) - represents the 7 stars; the 7
churches; which is a picture of Jesus our high priest in
heaven, making intercession for us. Just like the high priest in
the ancient temple would sacrifice the bull for the atonement
of sin!
The Eagle (Aquila) - represents **Christ** that seas above all
principalities and powers.
The Lion (Leo) - again represents Jesus the Lion of the Tribe
of Judah.

- **The Hale-Bopp Comet** - was first discovered in 1995
because it very rarely passes the earth. It's much brighter
than Haley's comet. On 7/23/1995 it was spotted inside
Sagittarius (half beast/half man).
   In 1998 it exited out of Orion during the Feast of Pentecost.
The war on terror started 4 years later. When a comet passes
Orion it is believed to be a sign of the end of an age.
   Astronomers have determined that prior to the mid 1990's
Hale-Bopp was last seen 4200 years ago when Noah was

building the ark! "As it was in the days of Noah, so it will be at
the coming of the Son of Man." **Mathew 24:37**
- To Hebrew scholars 1998 is a significant year. It is the
Hebrew year 5758. The 5 and 8 add up to the name of Noah.
They believe it indicates that 1998 began the seasons of
Noah. *"As it was in the days of Noah, so it will be at the
coming of the Son of Man."* Mathew 24:37

- A major prophetic event took place in 1967. On that year
Jerusalem was reunited with Israel during the infamous six
day war. *From 1967 forward, astronomers have observed
an increase in cosmic activity,* including but not limited to
increased sunspot activity, the lunar landing in 1969 and the
shoemaker levy comet strike.

- *"Crown of Thorns Galaxy"* This galaxy was discovered in
2009 by the Hubble telescope that looks just like the crown
that was placed on Jesus head prior to His crucifixion. In the
center of this galaxy is a very bright star or object. I believe
that this is symbolic of Christ, who is the light of the world -
and this light is positioned right in the middle of the crown of
thorns! (Google it and see it for yourself!)

- *"Hand of God Nebula"* discovered by the Hubble space
telescope; it looks like a massive hand with fire shooting out of
its fingers! Could this be a sign of the coming tribulation
whereby the sequence of judgments includes fire coming
down from heaven?

The Star of Bethlehem:
During the birth of Jesus there was significant activity in the
heavens; both literally and physically. God may have created
a temporary new star called the star of Bethlehem. Perhaps
the star was a conjunction of Jupiter and Saturn which history
has signified major event. It could also have been a comet.
Such a comet was observed in 5 BC in China. There was
also a conjunction (joining of several stars) in 2 BC. All of

these incidents were happening during the time of Jesus birth. These alignments were for signs.
Upon Jesus death there was also a strange sign from heaven:
"From noon until three in the afternoon darkness came over all the land." **Mathew 27:45**
"The sun will be turned to darkness and the moon to blood before the coming of the great and glorious day of the Lord." <u>Acts 2:20</u>

<u>The significance of Numbers in the Bible</u>

Just like it is the foundation of all science and mathematics; numbers are also very significant in the bible. Of all the numbers, the number seven and multiples of seven is a very significant number. Seven is the number of completion. **Seven is a number that demonstrates how God is in charge of ALL things.**

<u>Here are just a few examples:</u>

- 7 days in the creation sequence
- God rested on the seventh day and made it Holy.
- 7 stars on Jesus right hands
- the 7 Lamp-stands - the 7 churches
- the 7 spirits of God
- the 7 oceans/seas
- The 7 major continents
- God established a year of jubilee (Leviticus 25:8-12), to take place every **49 years 7 x 7**, as a year to let the land rest and restore itself. Yes the earth is a living organism but it is not to be worshipped as some "green earth movement" folks do.
- From Exodus to the time Solomon dedicated the first Jewish Temple was 490 years or **70 x 7.**
- We see this very number at play again - from the dedication of the first Jewish temple (Solomon's temple) to the command of King Artaxerxes allowing the Jews to return to their land to rebuild Jerusalem again is **490 years (70 x 7)**

- Then again from the edict that allowed the Jews to return to their land and rebuild Jerusalem, to the Messiah Jesus is **490 years (70 x 7).** Do you see a trend here? Do you think this is coincidence?
- Preceding the millennium, there will be a seven year tribulation period (the Apocalypse), whereby the earth will be sanctified with fire before the return of Messiah.
- The **tribulation period lasts 7 years** (Read: "Revelation Mysteries Decoded: Unlocking the Secrets of the Coming Apocalypse)
- The tribulation will consist of 7 **seal judgments, 7 trumpet judgments and 7 bowl judgments**.
- Jesus addresses the seven churches of Asia in **Rev. 2-3**
- Our life revolves around a very structured seven day week, and God made it this way since the creation of man and this age (**Genesis 2:2**). We really cannot escape the significance of the number seven. The wise person is reminded of this every week of their life!

Important Note:

- Mankind has been given 6 days of one thousand years (**2 Peter 3:8**), and then there will be the last day of 1,000 years when the Messiah will rule the world during the millennium. During the 7th day - the 1000 year millennium, mankind will rest from Satan and sin; a one thousand year Sabbath, if you will.

   God's total plan for mankind revolves around the number seven. And the significance of this number is not just for Israel but for all mankind. Seven is God's number of completion, and the seventh number is Holy (i.e. the Sabbath day of rest). God made us in his image - God is Holy! **Genesis 1:26.** The number seven is indeed the number of God. Our destiny should we choose is to be Holy children of God through perpetuity!

Note: the number 6 is the number of man. Interestingly, man's body is composed of six main parts, a head, torso, 2 arms and 2 legs.

Other Numbers of significance in the Bible:

The Number twelve is quite significant also, it is the number of government:
- the 12 apostles
- the 12 tribes of Israel
- the 12 major constellations
- the 12 signs of the zodiac
- 12 pearly gates and foundations in heaven
- 12 months in a year.

The number 3 is the number of divinity. For example:
- The Trinity consists of Father, Son, and Holy Ghost
- Jesus was resurrected from the dead in 3 days

The number 6 is the number of man.
- Interestingly, man's body is composed of six main parts, a head, torso, 2 arms and 2 legs.
- Also mans allotted time on earth is 6,000 years,
- man is to work just 6 days (and rest on the seventh)
- and the Antichrist who will come out of the nations (a human being) is assigned the number 666.
The reason that I bring this up is because numbers also play a role in confirming certain signs. For example we see that the Zodiac consists of Twelve constellations, and each constellation has 3 Decans - that is right all twelve have exactly 3 Decans each. Then of course the fact that man was given 6,000 years on earth indicates that the signs in the heavens, and the coming Blood Moons may be pointing that the time of the end of this age may indeed be just around the corner.

Chapter 17 - The Final Call!

The Correlation behind Israel and the World

It is important that you understand that what happens to Israel, is an indication of what happens to the world as a whole. Hence the signs of the Zodiac and the coming Blood Moons in no way are isolated messages to Israel - even though tiny Israel will play a major role in the end day prophecies, just as it is playing today.

Just because His own (the Jews) rejected Him as their Messiah, does not negate the fact that Christ is indeed the true Messiah. The Jews wanted a Messiah that would liberate them from Roman authority, but just like carnal man, they were not interested in liberating their hearts from sin.

As a result their eyes were blinded to that one person that could have freed them from not just their national bondage, but from their spiritual bondage. God's chosen (Israel) has paid a great price for their rejection - and we are a witness to the great price that their rejection has reaped over the past 2000 years.

It seems as if the world - the Gentile Nations (a symbol of sin throughout the Old Testament) want to destroy Israel (symbolic of God). This everlasting hatred has deep and old roots (the serpent's hatred towards the woman). When nations hate and try to divide Israel up, they are doing so either out of ignorance of the word of God, rejection of the God of Abraham, Isaac and Jacob - or both!

It is a testament of God's Sovereignty that tiny Israel - a nation the size of New Jersey, has managed to survive despite being surrounded by enemies that have been seeking her destruction since its original formation and after it was re-established in 1948. There should be no doubt that the hand of God is protecting Israel in these last days.   Among its sworn enemies are Syria, Iran, and Egypt (all surround Israel). **Just as God protects little Israel, Jesus protects his church from the fiery darts (spiritual attacks) of the devil!**

But the prophecies declare that God will not allow Israel's destruction this time. This is the same God that today defends Israel from its many enemies (**Zechariah 12:8**). Only time will prove God's promise that once re-established, Israel will NOT be driven into the Ocean or Nuked into oblivion. **In the book of Revelation it becomes very clear that those who will be obliterated are those nations who try to destroy God's holy land in the time of the end**.

Yes just like the Messiah Jesus, Israel is hated and despised by many. Yet little do they know that Israel is actually a representation of the world. The religious self righteous should not point the finger at Israel - but rather on themselves! There is a little bit of Israel in all of our hearts for we are all children of Abraham. We are all rebellious in heart.

Israel is a reflection of what all mankind (especially the self righteous) has done from time memorial. Man (Jew and Gentile alike) has stubbornly rejected the Lord and has chosen the carnal way of living. **Thankfully for all of us judgment is reserved to the God of heaven, not to mortal man who cannot judge righteously!**

Notwithstanding, the lesson from Israel is that we can avoid the same consequences, when we also acknowledge what the heavens have been declaring since the beginning of the age - that Messiah Jesus Christ is Lord and savior of this world...

"He came to His own, and His own did not receive Him. But as many as received Him, to them He gave the

right to become children of God, to those who believe in His name: John 1:11-12

The good news is that in the time of the end, even Israel will finally acknowledge Christ as their Messiah. God never rejected them or us, even though they and most of mankind have rejected Him. A perfect parent never stops loving their children, regardless how obstinate they may be. How much more will a loving God who created us in His image, and Israel as the apple of His eye, patiently wait for us to open the door of our hearts and let Him in. Rest assured as kingdom come, just before the time of the end Israel will finally recognize Jesus Christ as their Messiah - it is written and most assuredly it will happen:

"And they will dwell safely there, build houses, and plant vineyards; yes, they will dwell securely, when I execute judgments on all those around them who despise them. Then they shall know that I am the Lord their God." Ezekiel 28:26

"For thus says the Lord of hosts: "He sent Me after glory, to the nations which plunder you; for he who touches you touches the apple of His eye." Zechariah 2:8

The Secret behind the "Tree of Life"

There were three types of trees in the Garden of Eden. Three trees in the Midst of the Garden:

1) All of the trees representative of all mankind
2) The Tree of the Knowledge of Good and Evil (in the midst of the Garden)
3) The Tree of Life (also located in the midst of the Garden)

Satan is pictured as the Tree of the Knowledge of Good and Evil, since this tree is represents sin, the carnal mind, and death.

Jesus is pictured as the Tree of Life - since He is the Light and the life of the world. This tree represents being spiritually minded and eternal life.

So right at the cradle of civilization the message was made clear that this entire age would be a battle for the soul of mankind; and the destiny of mankind would be sealed based on the choice made by our first parents!

But, falling prey to the serpent's cunning, man chose to eat first from the Tree of the Knowledge of Good and Evil. Upon making that choice they were evicted from the Garden of Eden since sin could not remain in the Garden, and carnally minded man could not have access to the Tree of Life.

Had they eaten of the Tree of life instead of disobeying God's commandment they would have lived forever. The tree of life would have given them the only knowledge that they really needed to have; divine knowledge directly from God!

So Instead of an immortal body, their body became mortal and subject to decay and death. They did gain carnal knowledge, but that knowledge would ensure a life of bondage to Satan, whereby the spirit would have to constantly struggle against the lusts of the flesh, and all other types of temptations associated with the carnal mind.

BUT the great news is that today, once again, you can have access to the Tree of Life, and secure eternal life! The Tree of Life now can reside inside all of those who accept Jesus Christ as their Lord and savior. Its fruit is the Holy Spirit. **The Spirit of Jesus (the Holy Spirit) can balance our scales!** *__The Tree of Life is a symbol of Christ__*! The tree of life is the Spirit--the mind of Christ. "To be spiritually minded IS LIFE

Below are scriptural references confirming this truth:

"I am the living bread which came down from heaven. If anyone eats of this bread, he will live forever; and the bread that I shall give is My flesh, which I shall give for the life of the world." John 6:51

"Whoever eats My flesh and drinks My blood has eternal life, and I will raise him up at the last day." **John 6:54**

"For to be carnally minded is death, but to be spiritually minded is life and peace." Romans 8:6

"For if you live according to the flesh you will die; but if by the Spirit you put to death the deeds of the body, you will live." Rom. 8: 13

"He who eats My flesh and drinks My blood abides in Me, and I in him." John 6:56
"I am the vine, you are the branches. He who abides in Me, and I in him, bears much fruit; for without Me you can do nothing." **John 15:5**

The Final Call

As I close this final chapter, I feel compelled to urge you to heed God's call for your salvation. I truly believe we are already in the final chapter of the age of mankind! *Let's heed the message behind the constellation Argo, the third Decan in the house of Cancer; it is time to board Jesus ship of salvation, before it leaves for home! Once it leaves it will be too late and you will be left behind!*

We are all sinners and come short of the glory of God. And God can turn all sinners into saints in His eyes - and He will remember their sins no more. Therefore we must not judge anyone other than ourselves. A message of the Gospels and the book of Revelation is that justice must and will be executed by He that is sinless and unblemished. Only merciful Jesus is worthy and fair enough to judge mankind righteously. Only the creator knows what is inside the heart of His creation!

The spirit leads me to write what Jesus wrote on the ground before the crowd that was prepared to stone Mary Magdalene, a prostitute. Jesus already knew that she would repent and that she would become one of His disciples. Because of her repentant heart at that pivotal moment in her life, ***What Jesus wrote on the ground - was her name in the "Lambs Book of Life"***!

While the Zodiac signs give us a picture of this age and the outcome thereof, the coming Blood moons warn us of impending Judgment. It is time to get our spiritual life in order. **Choose Life!**

This is YOUR pivotal moment in your life - it is still NOT too late to secure your name in the Lambs Book of Life! But the ship will soon leave the dock in its journey to Eternity!

Do you want to be a mere carnal mortal, held captive to the lusts of the flesh and sin - and to the whims of the dragon - that great serpent Satan? Or do you want to become the supernatural spirit filled being that God designed you to be - destined to a glorious resurrected body for eternity? It is your choice. ***Choose life***!

Friends, when you accept Jesus as your Lord and savior, at that moment the Kingdom of God is within you **(Luke 17:21).**

When you activate your spirit mind empowered by God's Holy Spirit, then will the universe inside of you come to life and open the portal to heaven - which secures eternal life!

May this book be a source of inspiration for you, having awakened the inner depths of your soul, so that you develop an unquenchable desire to seek the truth found in the word of God - **the Holy Bible** so that you too may wisely choose to become one of the sons of the Lord, and join all His children at the soon coming **Marriage Supper of the Lamb**...

"Then he said to me, "Write: 'Blessed are those who are called to the marriage supper of the Lamb!'" And he said to me, "These are the true sayings of God." Revelation 19:9

"Behold, I am coming quickly! Blessed is he who keeps the words of the prophecy of this book." Revelation 22:7

May God guide you in your journey through life.

<u>Bonus Chapter</u>:

This complimentary chapter is an excerpt (chapter 7) from my brand new book published on 1/1/2015:
"Apocalypse Countdown - 2015 to 2021"

Chapter 7 - The Book of Revelation and the Apocalypse

While the prior chapter was date specific relative to heavenly signs and appointed feast days that could be harbingers of the apocalypse. We will now discover the events and the series of judgments that will unfold once the apocalypse begins.

The book of Revelation is appropriately the last book of the bible, because it is primarily the **go to book on the last days of this age**. It also is the revelation of Jesus Christ in that it reveals that Jesus Christ was and is the Messiah, and He will return to rule the world at the conclusion of this age of man. God allowed man 6,000 years to mess everything up and prove that **without the Spirit of God** mankind has always and will always be unable to resist the temptations of their carnal spirit which makes them susceptible to the cunning of Satan and his dark evil influences, which has and will ultimately lead this world to its demise.

To stay in topic let's review the key clues in the book of Revelation regarding the apocalypse and what types of events are revealed to take place before during and after the great tribulation period (apocalypse).

The apostle John was in exile in the Island of Patmos by the Romans because of his testimony of Jesus. While in exile, he received many visions from Jesus and some of His angels. John could only describe these visions symbolically as they were for the last days; the days that you and I live in. So the description of these visions can be quite confusing to the untrained mind. Since my book is about the time of the end I will only cover the key prophecies of Revelation pertaining to our time.

Before we begin, keep in mind that in many end time prophecies duality comes into play, representing visions and prophecies that may apply to more than one nation, time in history, and meaning. For example when one reads of Babylon, it may refer to ancient Babylon or to Babylon of the last days. With careful study and cross referencing of scriptures, you can and will correctly interpret the prophecies. With that said let's move on to the phases of judgments during the apocalypse.

Rev. Chapter 6 and 7 - Jesus has a scroll in his hand with 7 seals. When He opens the seals of the scroll - each one announces the Judgments that are to come upon the whole earth. The first four scrolls reveal the four horsemen of the apocalypse. These are not literal men riding on horses but rather they are symbolic of the events that will be unfolding during the great tribulation (apocalypse). I believe these events will occur in rapid succession one after another; hence the vision of horses in motion; one immediately after the other.

The Seven Seal Judgments

The 1st Seal is the first horse - a white horse whose rider has a bow but no arrows. This may be describing **the Antichrist** (man of perdition) that is to come, masquerading as a savior with peaceful intentions, and thus conquering an unsuspecting world through deceptive means (**Rev. 6:2**).

The 2nd Seal is the second horse - a rider on a red horse carrying a great sword to take peace from the earth, **so that people could kill one another.** This is clearly symbolizing war among the nation - perhaps **World War III (Rev. 6:4).**

The 3rd Seal is the third horse - a rider on a black horse carrying scales on his hand and based on what is said in this passage, it is revealing **a great famine throughout the world**; a great shortage of food supplies as a result of devastated lands due to the war released by the second seal (**Rev. 5-6**)

The 4th Seal is the fourth horse - a rider on an ashen (grayish green) horse symbolizing death and hell.   This rider is **symbolic of the beast kingdom consisting of the ten nation confederacy.** Notice that the rider is referring to "*them*" and not "*him*". It further states that "power was given to them over a fourth of the earth, to kill with sword, with hunger, with death, and the beasts of the earth." I believe this fourth rider is the final beast kingdom under control of the man of perdition that destroys 1/4th of the earth - possibly with weapons of mass destruction! I believe that the "**beasts of the earth**" is NOT referring to lions, bears and other predator animals but rather the leaders of the beast kingdom, consisting of the ten nation confederacy and the henchmen that martyr the saints as we read in the fifth seal that follows.

Note: The term "***beast***" refers to the beast kingdom and all the people that associate with it, and who worship the beast (Satan) and take his mark (the mark of the beast).

5th Seal - reveals a great persecution and Martyrdom of a myriad of saints by the beast kingdom because of their testimony/witness of the name of Jesus Christ as the son of God in accordance with the word of God, in the Holy bible. These who are referred to as "**saints**" are the Christians and elect who are beheaded or killed by other means because they do not bow down and worship the Antichrist (Satan's man of perdition), who has come to full power over the earth after the fourth seal above.

Important Note: The revelation clearly reveals that the saints (all Christians - the body of Christ) will be targeted and hated not just by the one world government but most of the inhabitants of the world who will be brainwashed into believing that the antichrist is God, and the false prophet is Jesus! That is why they will gladly take the mark of the beast. This hatred towards all witnesses of the Lord is clearly revealed in various places including **Rev. 11:10**, when the inhabitants of the earth celebrate when the two witnesses appointed by God to witness to the world in an effort to save as many souls as possible, are killed by the man of perdition (Satan's representative on earth).

6th Seal - A great Earthquake rocks the planet.

7th Seal - when the seventh seal is released, there is silence in Heaven for 1/2 hour, and seven angels are given seven trumpets in preparation of the release of the trumpet judgments of God. This appears to be a transition point, a short period of rest, perhaps to allow for some to repent before the trumpet judgments begin.

NOTE: This period of rest at the seventh seal is interesting when we consider that the Lord rested on the seventh day and sanctified it (made it Holy), and how he commands you and I to do the same. Obviously the Sabbath day was never abolished as it is symbolically observed even in heaven during the apocalypse, and it is one of the Ten Commandments (**Exodus 20:8-11**). This may be another main reason why the **seventh seal** does not release any judgments upon the earth! When you study Revelation carefully as I have, you will perceive the level of perfect precision on how even the last seven years of the age of man unfold. It is like a religious or holy ceremony in heaven commemorating the end of this imperfect age.

The first 6 seals of Revelation chapter six appear to be a synopsis of the key events that will occur during the great tribulation, which **will NOT begin** until the man of perdition is finally revealed.

Note that these seal judgments are not necessarily direct judgments from God, but rather judgments and curses that man has brought upon himself by placing their faith in man, instead of in God!

The Seven Trumpet Judgments

Now let's move on to the seven trumpet judgments:
The trumpet Judgments are sounded by seven Angels. These angels are charged with executing God's judgments; the "wrath of God judgments". We can infer from **Rev. 6:10-11** that these judgments come upon the earth in large part because of the blood of the saints (God's children, the body of Christ) that was shed because of their testimony of God's word:

1) The first angel sounded his trumpet - which destroys all green grass, and _a third_ of all trees. (**Rev. 8:7**). This would obviously lead to a global famine, and many millions would die of starvation.

So the **first trumpet** appears to be describing a thermonuclear attack that destroys a third of earth (Note that the western hemisphere is one third of the earth). *A third of the trees* were burned up as well as all green grass. One can imagine the enormous loss of life and the magnitude of the pestilence and famine that would affect the entire earth when one third of all trees are vaporized and **_all green grass_** (i.e. vegetation) is burned up.

2) The second angel sounds his trumpet and a great mountain falls on the sea and a third of the sea became blood. This is NOT a literal mountain or literal blood, but is John's way of describing perhaps **a large asteroid** or **nuclear missiles** that land in the ocean and contaminate one third of the ocean water. As a direct result, **_one third_** of all sea creatures perish, and one third of the ships at sea are destroyed. Most likely tsunamis will also wreak havoc on many coastal areas (**Rev. 8:8-9**).

3) When the third angel sounds his trumpet - a great star fell from heaven burning like a torch, and this one contaminates **one third** of the rivers and springs of water, many men perish from drinking this water. This one may be caused by nuclear weapons (or again asteroids), because the description "burning like a torch" is more descriptive of an intercontinental ballistic missile (ICBM), and it contaminates drinking water, causing many people die from drinking it. Perhaps they are not aware of the level of radiation in this water thinking that the contamination is not so widespread (**Rev. 8:10-11**).
So this star is most likely one or several nuclear missiles impacting a land mass with rivers and springs of water. We also read here that a third of the earth is darkened due to this nuclear attack on an area of the globe, resulting in great death.

4) The fourth angel sounded and "*a third* of the sun, moon, and stars were struck, so that a third of them were darkened and a third of the day did not shine (**Rev. 8:12**). This must mean that one third of the earth has been devastated either by a massive asteroid impact or thermo-nuclear exchange or related catastrophe.

Make note that so far *one third* of the earth's land mass is affected by the first four trumpet blasts? God is placing great emphasis on this, which leads me to believe that the great tribulation will begin when a large land and ocean area of the world is devastated.

In **Rev. 8:13** we are warned that the next 3 trumpet judgments are going to make things even worse for the remaining inhabitants of the earth.

Note: Given the **Rev. 8:13** warning, it is hard to imagine as I write this in early December 2014, how progressively bad things will actually get. This is **_probably because at this point the restrainer is removed_** from the earth giving Satan power to wreak maximum havoc over this planet.
We should all **_pray_** that God indeed will rapture His elect - the church (the body of Christ) before the great tribulation begins, as many theologians believe (Pre-tribulation rapture)! But when we read in the revelations that a myriad (millions) of saints will be martyred during the apocalypse, one must wonder and prepare for a mid or post rapture of the saints. Regardless, we must remain prepared and ready since our appointed time to meet our maker can be at any moment.

5) The fifth angel sounds his trumpet - A Star (perhaps a fallen angel) falls from heaven and has been given the key to the bottomless pit (Hades/hell). He opens the bottomless pit and smoke arose out of the pit like the smoke of a great furnace (**Rev. 9:1-2**). This may be describing a massive volcanic eruption which also shoots out smoke just like a great furnace!

The fifth trumpet also releases evil spirits from Hades who afflict all men except the 144,000 who have the seal of God on their forehead and who have been granted special protection from God (**Rev. 9:3-11**).

The locusts that arise out of the bottomless pit as a result of the fifth trumpet could be some form of **germ warfare** or **manufactured virus** since they do not harm the vegetation but only the inhabitants of the earth; specifically those who do not have the seal of God on their forehead (i.e. the 144,000). This germ or virus apparently affects the body for five months; perhaps a vaccine is developed to curtail the pandemic. Jesus does warn in **Mathew 24**, that the end of day judgments will include pestilence and disease (such as the Ebola virus outbreak of 2014).

Note: The revelation that demons are instructed to afflict only the non-believers, should be a reminder to all that Satan is NOT even a friend to the non-believers. Satan does not discriminate, he hates anything associated with God and equally, and is bent on destroying it all and taking it all to hell with him. This includes the grass, trees, planet earth and all human beings which were all created in the image of God.

6) The sixth angel sounds his trumpet - and four **_fallen_** Angels which were bound at the Euphrates River are released (**Rev. 9:14-15**). These evil angelic beings were so powerful that they had to be physically restrained until this moment in time.

The Euphrates River runs through Iraq. This may be indicating that the area of Iraq (where the terror army called ISIS is presently based), and the Middle East as a whole may be ground zero for the establishment of the beast kingdom and headquarters of the man of perdition. Also interesting how this area of the Middle

East has always been an area of Jewish and Christian intolerance and persecution.

These four fallen angels kill a third of mankind, with a massive 200,000,000 man army which once the demonic influences are released in that region, invade from the east.

They are able to do this by influencing an army of 200 million; this may be a continuation or beginning of World War III that was announced at the opening of the aforementioned second and fourth seals.

Note: In John's time an army that size was impossible. Today it is quite possible considering the nearly seven billion worldwide population. We also discover that this army will kill one third of mankind with the use of weapons that rain down fire and brimstone **which again reads to me like nuclear weaponry (Rev. 9:15-18)**.

Rev. 9:20-21 makes it clear why these judgments continue to persist to the very end, as those who survive through all of the prior judgments still refuse to repent from worshipping demons, idols, sorcery, murder, sexual immorality and thefts.

The seventh angel sounds his trumpet and we have another break from the Judgments; **_another Sabbath break_** in between the trumpet and the final bowl judgments. Victory is proclaimed in heaven and a celebration commences as the angels and elders announce that the kingdoms of this world are now the kingdoms of the Lord; as the Messiah prepares for His triumphant second coming!

The Sabbath is to be a day where we stop all work and worship the Lord; thanking Him for the prior week's blessings. On this day we pray, nourish our spirit with the word, and develop our relationship with the Lord. We saw that after the sixth seal was released, Revelation chapter seven is an instructional chapter. Once again after the sixth trumpet judgment in Revelation chapter nine, chapter ten is also an instructional chapter right through Rev. 11 verse 14 when the seventh trumpet judgment is released.

After the seventh trumpet judgment, Revelation chapters 12 through 15 are instructional chapters as well which describe the following:

Rev. Ch. 12: This chapter covers the cosmic battle that Satan has waged against Israel, and mankind. Note that he is NO MATCH to Jesus and God, so that he can only attempt to defeat Jesus and God through mankind! ***Satan knows he already lost his battle against the Messiah almost 2,000 years ago when Jesus Christ became our sacrificial Lamb at the cross, allowing anyone who acknowledges and accepts His sacrifice the right to become children of the Most High***! Messiah has **already** earned the deed to planet earth and the universe. In His mercy He is just waiting for the full number of saved souls to be reached before He returns (**Rev. 6:10-11**)!

Rev. Ch. 13: This chapter describes the antichrist, false prophet and the beast kingdom that will reign approximately three and one half years before the second coming.

Rev. Ch. 14 and 15: are celebratory chapters in heaven whereby the angels and the saints (all those who were previously martyred because they refused the mark of Satan) prepare for the final series of judgments and the return of the Messiah to establish a new heaven and a new earth - one that is purified, and cleansed of all sin). Some scholars believe that by this point the rapture may have already occurred.

The Final Seven Bowl Judgments

Now we move on to the last series of judgments; the Bowl (also referred to as vial) judgments. Like the Trumpet judgments, the bowl judgments are also a part of the **"Wrath of God Judgments"**. This series of judgments appears to be particularly for those who accepted the mark of Satan (mark of the beast), and all who refuse to repent.

1) The first Bowl is poured out and a horrible sore *afflicts all those who took the mark of the beast (Satan) and who worshiped his image*.
I hope that you like I are finding it really hard to comprehend how so many will be so deceived by Satan in these last days into thinking that this coming demon possessed one world government leader of the final one world government is God or can actually defeat and or prevent the second coming of Messiah.

2) The second bowl is poured out on the sea and it became blood (contaminated). This time all the living creatures of the sea are dead (not just one third).

3) <u>The third bowl is poured</u> on all rivers and springs of water so that no drinkable water remains.

4) <u>The fourth bowl is poured out</u> and the sun scorches men with fire. Perhaps the ozone layer fails amidst all the level of contamination and radiation in the atmosphere.

5) <u>The fifth bowl</u> immerses the beast kingdom (the one world empire) in total darkness. I perceive that since with the fourth bowl there is a sun that scorches men with fire the sun now fries out the electrical grid (**Rev. 16:10-11**)

6) <u>The sixth bowl</u> dries up the Euphrates River which allows an army from the east (king of the East) the ability to cross over to engage in the **battle of Armageddon** along with other invading armies. This last battle is referred to as "**the great day of God Almighty**" (**Rev. 16:14**), probably because it brings an end to the age of man.

On or around the battle of Armageddon the Lord returns as we read in the verse that follows:

<u>Rev. 16:15</u>

"Behold, I am coming as a thief. Blessed is he who watches, and keeps his garments, lest he walks naked and they see his shame."

7 the seventh bowl judgment: After the seventh bowl judgment is poured out on the air a great voice declares ***"it is done"*** which releases the greatest earthquake in history. It must break the Richter scale along with everything else since the force of this quake collapses mountains and Islands.

This massive earthquake is the final event of the age of man as the remaining chapters of Revelation are instructional as follows:

Revelation 17 & 18: These are two very important prophecy chapters that describe who or what **"Babylon the Great"** is. This great entity is so important to end time events that God dedicates two full chapters to this topic. This will be covered in detail in another chapter.

Rev. 19: Describes the Messiah's second coming, with Jesus returning with His heavenly army to put an end to Satan and his minions. It also describes the Marriage Supper of the Lamb.

Rev. 20: Describes the Judgment of the antichrist, false prophet, Satan, the demons, zombies (sorry, I couldn't help it!), and all those who took the mark of the beast.

Rev. Chapter 21 - Describes the new Heavens and new earth - our glorious new home through eternity!

In Chapter 22: The revelation of Jesus Christ culminates in His words:

"I, Jesus, have sent my angel to give you this testimony for the churches. I am the Root and the Offspring of David, and the bright Morning Star."

My brothers and sisters in the Lord, as you now know, many prophetic signs are converging in 2015, making it quite possible that 2015 may be the harbinger year, warning that the apocalypse is imminent. So I believe that this book is one of the most important publications that I have ever penned.

Among the many crucial end time prophecies and topics that you will discover in Apocalypse Countdown - 2015 - 2021 are:

- Discover all of the key prophecies from all of the great ancient prophets; the key signs of the time of the end
- 2015 - the Harbinger Year
- Where is America in Bible Prophecy?
- The rise of America
- The coming fall of America
- Who is Babylon the Great - America?
- Why will Babylon the Great be Destroyed?
- Who will Destroy Babylon the great?
- How will Babylon the Great be Destroyed?
- Where will the antichrist establish his headquarters
- What nations will comprise the ten nation end time Empire
- Why is Jerusalem such a Burdensome Stone?
- What are the Consequences of Dividing up God's Land?
- The mystery of the Shemita blessings and curses.
- The Jubilee year connection
- The month of September and its link to financial and national disasters.
- Why there is more to 9/11 than most think?
- The coming seven trumpet judgments
- Who is the Beast of Revelation?
- Who is the 666 - the antichrist?

- Why will so many take the Mark of the Beast?
- The antichrist will come out of which Nation?
- Who are the Kings of North and South?
- Where is "Satan's throne" located?
- Left behind? What the prophecies reveal about the Rapture
- How to Survive the Coming Apocalypse
- Apocalypse Survival supplies and tips
- Emergency Supplies
- How to Prepare Emotionally and Mentally
- And more!

Again, I am not saying that 2015 is the year, but rather that from 2015 to 2021 we may indeed experience such great unrest and calamities throughout the world as discussed in this book, so that the controlling majority who are **void of the spirit of the living God** will force an unholy union in hopes for security. Tragically the security they secure will be a false security strait from hell!

This was a complimentary chapter from my new release:

"Apocalypse Countdown - 2015 to 2021"

Get Complimentary Access to: "Prophecy Alerts"

Dear Reader: Prophecies are being fulfilled so rapidly in these last days that I am offering my readers complimentary access to "*prophecy alerts*" so that you get "*Breaking Prophecy News*" as soon as it breaks...Just follow this link below and sign Up today...

http://robertritebooks.com/prophecy-alerts/

About Robert Rite
Robert Rite is the author of several books including:

- "Apocalypse Countdown - 2015 to 2021"

- "Apocalypse Codes - Decoding the Prophecies in the Book of Daniel"

- "100 Proofs that the Bible is the Inspired Word of God and Scientifically Accurate"

- "Ancient Apocalypse Codes"

- "Awaken the Supernatural You!"

- "Aliens, Fallen Angels, Nephilim and the Supernatural"

- "Babylon the Great is Fallen, is Fallen! Who is "Mystery Babylon" of the End of Days?"

- "Blood Moons Rising"

- "Be healed!....How to Unlock the Supernatural Healing Power of God"

- "Bible Verses for Supernatural Blessings"

- End of Days

- "God, Mystery Religions, Cults, and the coming Global Religion"

- "Prophecies of the Apocalypse: Unlocking the End Time Prophetic Codes as Revealed by the Ancient Prophets"

- "Revelation Mysteries Decoded: Unlocking the Secrets of the coming Apocalypse"

- "The New Age Movement vs. Christianity: and the Coming Global Religion"

- "Unlocking the Supernatural Power of Prayer"

- "128 Powerful Bible Verses that can Save Your Life!"

Most recently Robert has released "End of Days" which is part of the "Supernatural Series" of books.

Robert is also the creator of over 135 articles on bible facts, and end-of-day mysteries and prophecies among other related topics. Visit Robert at RobertRiteBooks.com for sample chapters, press releases and related information.

Says Robert Rite:
"It is said that the truth at times is more stimulating than fiction. So have the best of both worlds, and stimulate your mind and soul with subject matter - that really matters"

Robert Rite's - Social Profiles:
Blog URL's:
http://RobertRiteBooks.com
http://Bible-Blog.org

Amazon Author Page: http://www.amazon.com/-/e/B00GOGIBEG

Facebook Page:
https://www.facebook.com/robertritebooks

Robert Rite at Twitter
Twitter Handle: @robertrite

Google Plus URL:
https://plus.google.com/u/0/100112453810665259776/posts/p/pub

Made in the USA
Monee, IL
20 April 2021

66255990R00085